John McAslan & Partners stands out among the newer British architectural practices for its inventiveness, versatility and commitment to the art of architecture. Although the work of the McAslan studio has foundations in a sense of history, it retains a zest and a thirst for innovation and radical thinking that evoke the spirit of the heroic days of modern architecture. At the heart of the practice, however, is the will to build. McAslan's major projects of the 1990s reflect a belief in the rational and the practical – not to say the pragmatic. Perhaps uniquely among architects of his generation, McAslan has built in Europe, Japan and the USA, as well as Britain.

A Scot by birth but a Londoner by habit, John McAslan trained at Cambridge Seven Associates (C7A) in Boston before joining the Richard Rogers office in the heady days of the early 1980s and then going on to found Troughton McAslan in 1984 (with Jamie Troughton). His architecture has long developed from the High-Tech mould and is increasingly exploring the iconography of modern design. Wright, Mendelsohn and Kahn are among McAslan's references – an inspiration and a source of renewal, McAslan believes, for a late twentieth-century architecture over-obsessed with stylistic considerations.

McAslan's concern for history has led his studio into rehabilitation and adaptative projects for classic Modernist icons – the De La Warr Pavilion at Bexhill-on-Sea and the Peter Jones store in London, for example, not to mention Wright's extraordinary campus at Florida Southern College. Working with the past is second nature to the practice, but McAslan's central concern is a timeless one: insistence on the proper use of materials and the creative use of space and form. He has been characterized as an empiricist, but the term is too constrictive. McAslan seeks to make an honest, accesible modern architecture for the twenty-first century, rooted in the past but looking to the future.

JOHN McASLAN

 Thames & Hudson

I would like to thank all those who have
collaborated with our practice since I began this
adventure in 1984, notably my colleagues past and
present (in particular Jamie Troughton) and our
long-suffering clients and consultants. Most of all
I'm indebted to Dava, Hannah, Renwick and Flora,
without whose love and support heaven only
knows what I'd be up to.
John McAslan, London, September 1999

First published in the United Kingdom in 1999 by
Thames & Hudson Ltd, 181A High Holborn,
London WC1V 7QX

British Library Cataloguing-in-Publication Data
A catalogue record for this book is available from
the British Library

ISBN 0-500-28174-2 CN

Designed by Thomas Manss & Company
Printed and bound in Singapore by C.S. Graphics

John McAslan & Partners

Buildings and Projects

Appendix

From Survival to Success by Martin Pawley   The studio of John McAslan & Partners is at the north end of Kensington Church Street in London's West End, at the hinge of genteel Kensington and raffish Notting Hill. John McAslan once came perilously close to moving to Southwark, but, aware of the advantages of continuity as well as stability, he looks set to remain in Kensington Church Street for a long time to come. He also lives near by.   **McAslan's studio** is a machine for working in. There is a small reception area inside the door and beyond that a large conference room, furnished with an assemblage of white tables surrounded by Eames chairs and architectural models. Past this is the studio, where thirty or so people work in an environment packed with drawings, more models and advanced computer equipment. Everything in the low-ceilinged but amply daylit space is white except the silver-grey venetian blinds and the blue computer monitors. The only evidence of hierarchy is a bank of white storage cabinets left of centre, which looks strong enough to repel a ram raider (it is referred to as 'Hadrian's Wall'); beyond it are three alcoves, each one with a white table. From the middle alcove John McAslan runs his practice, currently responsible for a range of remarkable masterplanning and design projects in the United Kingdom and abroad totalling some £250 million worth of work at construction value.   **Born in** Glasgow in 1954, John McAslan was the son of a doctor who later taught in the United States, and the grandson on his mother's side of a Glasgow lawyer so devoted to his business that in his eighties he still went to his office every day. Both the American connections of his father and the dogged determination of his grandfather and his mother played a part in forming McAslan's career. The first set the course for his early professional life, the other two strongly suggest the origins of the resolve that has enabled him time and again to build a substantial commission out of the slenderest of possibilities.   **McAslan's working** practices, like those of all in his profession, were honed through his training under various architects. After stints at Cambridge Seven Associates (C7A) in Boston, McAslan worked with the Richard Rogers Partnership during the 1980s, an apprenticeship that – closely followed by C7A – has the greatest impact on his design philosophy. McAslan worked on a number of Rogers buildings during that period, including the Patscenter in Princeton, supervised by Pierre Botschi. To this day he recalls with admiration the way the dogged Swiss perfectionist intervened, time after time, to refine the detailing of the building up to the last possible moment. 'The people in the Rogers office were dedicated to their architecture,' he says. 'They would go to extremes over what seemed to me at the time to be peripheral details. They would do anything, go completely over the top if that was what it took, just to get things right. It was a struggle I only really appreciated later, when I was in practice for myself.'   **After a** fruitful partnership with Jamie Troughton that lasted from 1984 to 1996, McAslan established John McAslan & Partners, which has allowed him to develop and refine his design philosophy and approach. His firm has a more focused design ethic now, based on McAslan's conception of his own general overseeing role, which is injected with periods of intense participation. While he is heavily involved in every design project that comes into the office, he often places himself on the sidelines, adopting the role of an adviser who must occasionally lead from the front to ensure that the practice retains its unique identity.   **In 1999** John McAslan was appointed to a five-year professorship in the School of Architecture at the University of Wales in Cardiff, which also involves significant input from his practice associates. The position has begun to crystallize his view of a total architecture, embracing both new built forms and the adaptation of existing buildings. He believes that the sheer scale of the

industrial and commercial legacy of the past, coupled with the rise of conservation culture, is turning adaptive reuse into a new frontier within architecture itself. 'When you are working with existing buildings, part new, part old – especially with industrial buildings that have long spans and generous headroom – you come to realize that almost any building can be adapted. All over the world our work is increasingly going to involve dealing with decayed, underutilized, hugely altered buildings. In my view the answer is not just to restore them – often there is little that is authentic left to restore – but to adapt them, drastically if necessary. I like the American view of this challenge. In the United States they start off by saying: "Change what is there into something useful." My aim with students and in practice is to discuss the realities of designing operational buildings, masterplanning and adaptive reuse. To inspire them with respect for the demands of the advocacy work that is necessary in connection with so many of our schemes. I'd say that reuse, adaptability and extendibility are at least as important as designing perfect objects. I find there is a great deal of satisfaction to be gained from gutting old buildings, enabling them to breathe again and creating dramatic new usable space.' **John McAslan** would be the first to concede that architectural practice is a high-risk business. 'If you let things slide I guess you could lose everything,' is how he puts it. But he believes that survival brings experience and confidence. For him, learning when he has to demonstrate his skill and when it is not necessary to do so has enabled him to switch the maximum effort of his studio from one project to another to keep in time with these crucial moments. That way he can work with his small, highly motivated (young) team, rather than in a larger and more conventional practice arrangement. As for the so-called burden of advocacy and consultation, he thinks the results are worth the hours it takes. 'Going along to talk to community groups, the Twentieth Century Society, English Heritage or the like is often fundamental,' he says. 'Consultation avoids problems later. It helps prevent the victory of style over substance and gives you the confidence to create new architecture. After all, the greatest challenge in architectural practice is finding ways to express yourself creatively in what you do, and that, I believe, is a prize worth fighting for.'

The studio

Industrial ruin, Dundee

McAslan's primary references are from growing up in Scotland, its industrial past and contemporary character, which has produced a richly varied (and sometimes painful) cultural legacy.

Triptych, 1986, by Ken Currie

A Practice History by Kenneth Powell

John McAslan's formative period as an architect in the 1970s coincided with a time of crisis in British architecture – a crisis of confidence as the Modern movement, dominant since the Second World War, seemed to have lost direction or even 'lost out'. On a more mundane level, the oil crisis and recession in the West had hit architecture hard. New directions were proffered as the way ahead – neo-vernacular, community architecture, self-build, garbage architecture and Postmodernism among them. There was a sense of retreat, of pessimism. When the revival came, it produced an extraordinary variety of work. **When McAslan** came back to Britain in late 1979, after a period of training in the USA, he found the differences striking. In America modern architecture had a certain uniformity. By contrast, the work of such architects as Richard Rogers, Norman Foster, Jeremy Dixon and Terry Farrell highlighted the pluralism of the British scene. 'High-Tech', not just a source of renewal but the means whereby British architecture gained a new influence on the world scene, seemed to offer a viable way ahead. McAslan was nine years old when Team 4 Architects was formed, seventeen when Rogers & Renzo Piano won the competition to build the Pompidou Centre in Paris. The Pompidou Centre (1971-77), Foster's Willis Faber & Dumas building in Ipswich (1975) and the Hongkong and Shanghai Banking Corporation building, Hong Kong (1979-84) were part of the context of his education and his architectural coming-of-age. A quarter of a century on, the progenitors of these buildings remain towering figures in British architecture. McAslan, in turn, is a leading – even a representative – member of an identifiable post-High-Tech generation in Britain. Having learnt from the masters of that manner, he has gone on to forge his own approach to design. His beliefs are certainly completely modern, having, indeed, tangible roots and references in the Modernist canon, but his approach is untrammelled by dogma or, for

that matter, any overbearing layer of rhetoric. If there are preconceptions in the work of this generation, they are the result of an acceptance that the world has changed. Outside the experimental world of Zaha Hadid, Daniel Libeskind and others, architecture has to be direct, flexible and durable. At the same time as being functionally and commercially mainstream, architects have to offer something that is unique. **McAslan's work** has been characterized as empirical, purposeful, even pragmatic, the implication being that it eschews romantic gestures. There is some truth in this generalization, but it should not obscure the essential seriousness and high ambition, even idealism, of McAslan's architecture. Only now, at the turn of the century, is the diverse modern tradition, refuelled in the 1970s by Rogers and Foster, breaking out of the constraints of style and school to produce buildings in which integrity and response to human need and the *genius loci* are balanced by a pursuit of practical efficiency, economy and adaptability to an unpredictable future. John McAslan's delight in the nature of materials is obvious and provides a link beyond High-Tech to the architecture of the early twentieth century and even the nineteenth – to Pierre Chareau, Antoni Gaudí and Joseph Paxton. McAslan's relationship to history is clearly critical to any understanding of his architecture. **His first** encounters with the past happened north of the border. McAslan's Scottish roots are significant. He was born in Glasgow in 1954 and raised in Scotland, although he never practised architecture in his native land. He is no more a Scottish architect than Renzo Piano (a major influence on his work) is an Italian architect. Modern architecture in Britain has suffered since its earliest days from a constant parochialism, leavened only by the work of such émigrés as Erich Mendelsohn, Ernö Goldfinger and Berthold Lubetkin. Parochialism forms no part of McAslan's outlook. His points of reference extend in space across the globe and in time back over the last

USS Alabama
(from McAslan's collection of childhood images)

Industrial ruins, Scotland
(left Perth, right Gourock)

Parking garage, Venice

two centuries.   **It is hardly** fanciful, however, to see the potent Glasgow architectural cocktail – the essential urban rationalism of the Alexander Thomson tradition, tempered by the romantic spirit of James Salmon, Charles Rennie Mackintosh and other Free Style masters – as one of the sources of McAslan's architecture. As a boy McAslan became familiar with the vernacular buildings of Scotland: industrial ruins, tower houses and brochs. He loved drawing ('very badly') such monuments from an early age. But when he was sixteen he designed an 'ideal house' – what appears to be a fusion of the Scottish vernacular and Frank Lloyd Wright, 'an embarrassingly cosy prairie style', he says. Yet the design sounds oddly like a fanfare for his later career.   **For any** child growing up in the 1950s and early 1960s, the USA was a magical world, half glimpsed through films, television and magazines. McAslan acquired piles of American memorabilia from the American servicemen at the Holy Loch polaris base and was amazed by the images of a futuristic life that they contained – so different from the west of Scotland. He was probably set on going to and working in America even then, but first came university. He applied to study architecture at both Glasgow and Edinburgh but eventually chose the latter, entering the school in the autumn of 1972. His fondest memories of Edinburgh are of the friendships forged and of a number of impressive tutors, such as Malcolm Higgs (now former head of school at Canterbury), who supervised McAslan's thesis on a search for modernism based on traditional Scottish architecture.   **But Edinburgh** was insular and more than a little parochial. 'I felt stifled by the environment,' McAslan recalls. 'We had little idea of what was going on elsewhere and weren't encouraged to find out.' Edinburgh gave him his basic training but, like Norman Foster and Richard Rogers fifteen years earlier, he was to find his architectural philosophy in the USA. Initially, he worked there in summer vacations, a

junior assistant in a big office. He found much of American architecture 'inspirational' and was impressed by the camaraderie of American practices. This aspect of America was later reflected in his own style of running a studio. In fact, a great deal of what McAslan learnt and absorbed in the USA in the 1970s was to emerge in the work of John McAslan & Partners twenty years later.   **McAslan went** back to the USA in the 'uplifting' bicentennial year of 1976, criss-crossing the country in search of the iconic masterpieces he had read about at home and also the work of current practitioners. He saw Frank Lloyd Wright's Fallingwater (Bear Run, Pennsylvania, 1935–39) and was entranced by Louis Kahn's Yale Art Gallery and Mellon Center (New Haven, Connecticut, 1951–53, 1969–77, respectively) and his Richards Medical Research Laboratories (Philadelphia, Pennsylvania, 1957–65). Again, the influence of these buildings, submerged for a time under British High-Tech themes, was to re-emerge in his later work. A further lasting connection with the USA was forged when he met his future wife, Dava, who had been brought up in Syracuse, New York.   **McAslan's real** introduction to American practice came in 1978–79, when he spent eighteen months in the office of Cambridge Seven Associates (C7A) in Boston. 'It was an inspired studio,' he recalls – for its theoretical, artistic and strongly visual ethos – a tonic to someone who thought all architectural offices were like that of the late Basil Spence back in Scotland. McAslan had trained there for a time, finding the ambience utilitarian and distinctly uninspiring. With an American wife and a good job in the USA, McAslan might well have never come home. Like so many before him, he took to the straightforward, open, unhierarchical society of America – always congenial to Scots – and could have easily imagined staying.   **In 1979** Britain voted in Margaret Thatcher as prime minister. Some of the consequences were disturbing, destructive and even tragic. Yet the Thatcher government's policy of deregulation, allegedly

McAslan's early life in Dunoon fused 1960s American and Scottish popular cultures and blossomed into a love of architecture, notably the work of the Chicago School, Frank Lloyd Wright and Louis Kahn, reinforced by his studies in the USA from 1976.

Bobby Lennox, Celtic

Louis Kahn, Fort Worth

Muddy Waters, Chicago

Alexander Thomson's
Holmwood, Glasgow

Industrial ruin, Paisley, Scotland

From his student days in Boston at Cambridge Seven Associates (designer of the seminal United States Pavilion at Montreal with Buckminster Fuller), McAslan went on to complete his early training with Richard Rogers. He contributed to the design of Patscenter buildings in Cambridge and Princeton, before establishing his practice with Jamie Troughton in 1984. They completed their first commission – Design House – later in the same year.

modelled on that of the USA, provided a boost for the City of London and for the invisible economy of banking and finance. Richard Rogers's Lloyds building was already going up in the City, a symbol of its world dominance. The building made Richard Seifert's brand-new NatWest Tower (now the International Finance Centre) look very dated. The reviving economy brought a development boom and it was not only the established 'commercial' practices that benefited. The developer Stuart Lipton, for example, insisted that good architecture paid off commercially. McAslan was subsequently to work in the model business park that Lipton developed at Stockley Park, near Heathrow, west of London.   **Through a** friend, Judy Bing, at Cambridge Seven, John McAslan met Richard Rogers and his partner, John Young, in Boston. He had come, somewhat reluctantly, to the conclusion that he should return to Britain to complete his studies. This could be combined with work in an office and it seemed natural to apply to Rogers, an internationally acclaimed master, for a post. So McAslan entered the immensely stimulating world of High-Tech. The Rogers office, then at Princes Place, Holland Park, was a place of passage for many of the most promising young architects in London – such people as Jan Kaplicky, Alan Stanton, Eva Jiricna, Chris Wilkinson and David Chipperfield. It was an academy as much as a workplace, not to mention a socially desirable address, but there was serious work to be done. McAslan (inevitably) worked on Lloyds for a time – it took seven years to build. But his most important job was on the building for PA Technology (Patscenter) near Cambridge and a further project for the same client in Princeton.   **The long** saga of Lloyds, from the time in 1977 when the design won the competition to the opening of the building in 1986, typified to some degree the contradictions of High-Tech. It was of course a one-off, prestige building for an old City institution but the architects' passionate concern for detail underlined the degree to

which their approach was painstakingly craft-based – far removed, in fact, from the 'fast-track' American-style construction that underlay such heroic 1980s projects as Canary Wharf (Docklands) and Broadgate (City). McAslan recalls that the Rogers office in the 1980s was still rooted in hand production – there were no computers. He particularly remembers (with horror) the moment when he discovered, after several weeks of drafting, that he had drawn all elevations a bay short. But the creative, multidisciplinary atmosphere of the office – a sort of hierarchical democracy – was highly congenial, and the buildings that it produced were striking and innovative, distinguished by almost obsessive attention to detail, pursuit of quality and disinclination to compromise. Richard Rogers Partnership was the breeding ground for the new practices that would, some predicted, produce a true renaissance of architecture in Britain. One of these practices was Troughton McAslan.   **Jamie Troughton** is four years older than John McAslan. He had trained at Cambridge University and worked for Norman Foster before joining the Rogers team. McAslan found him 'a distinctive figure . . . even an oddball', but he was attracted by Troughton's sense of humour and 'disengaged' manner and could well imagine working with him. When Troughton quit Rogers (in 1982) to found his own practice – not an easy break, for Rogers inspires loyalty in his colleagues – McAslan quickly followed him. The Thatcherite revolution opened the way not only for Canary Wharf and Stockley Park – developments of an entirely new order – but also allowed for a liberalization of the planning system. Divisions between office and industrial use, increasingly irrelevant in an electronic age, were broken down. The 'B1' unit was born, typically a place where design, media or arts operations were conducted, more often than not in a refurbished rather than a new building. Many young 1980s practices cut their teeth on such jobs and Troughton McAslan

United States Pavilion, Montreal

Patscenter, Princeton

Significant adaptive projects in the late 1980s, such as the St Peter's Street Studios in Islington, informed by Pierre Chareau's seminal Maison de Verre, blossomed into important new schemes in the early 1990s, such as Apple Computers headquarters.

was no exception. **Design House** (p. 68), the firm's first built commission, used the site of a very ordinary 1950s car showroom at a road junction in Camden Town, north London. The budget for its conversion to a design company was not vast – 'about half the cost of a toilet pod at Lloyds', McAslan recalls – but a stylish, eye catching building was the outcome. Completed in 1984, Design House is externally restrained. The original frame was reclad in blue aluminium. The interior was more radically transformed, with a new mezzanine, exposed services – reflecting the High-Tech mood of the time – and a bold use of colour in the spirit of the Rogers office. It was a convincing start. **A similar** approach was seen in Troughton McAslan's next commission (p. 66), the conversion of a three-storey, concrete-framed warehouse in Shepherd's Bush into design studios. The building was strong and adaptable, but the challenge lay in organizing the space inside it, in tune with the new use, and in servicing it. The key move was to open up the interior by cutting away floors and creating a top-lit, triple-storey space at its centre – a new atrium that is the functional and social heart of the place. Services were housed in exposed ducting, which was deliberately made a dominant feature of the project, while new staircases and other insertions were rigorously industrial in feel. The project was very much McAslan's – and it indicated the direction of his future work, particularly with regard to adaptation and reuse. **For a** time, rehabilitation jobs of this kind were the main support of the Troughton McAslan office. The studio in St Peter's Street (1988, p. 56), reflects a gentler, more refined approach. The staircase and use of glass brick are echoes of the famous Maison de Verre in Paris. At Colebrooke Place (p. 52), Islington, the conversion project completed in 1990 carries refinement even further, with a mezzanine carried on columns of almost classical elegance. **Looking back** on this early work, McAslan concedes that it was broadly High-

Tech. 'It was a comfortable way of working,' he says, 'but it was more than just a style. We were working with very ordinary sheds and striving to give them clarity and quality and, of course, extended use. High-Tech, as the term was understood in the mid-1980s, later turned into something, McAslan believes, that was 'forced, precious, even rigid' – in some cases, it meant squeezing uses into a preconceived look. Yet the early buildings by Team 4 and Richard Rogers Partnership had a remarkable directness that stemmed from a clear expression of engineering and function, infused with joy in construction. **The High-Tech** influence – innovative, accretive and infinite – worked its way through Troughton McAslan's first new-build schemes. The headquarters designed for Allied Breweries at Burton-upon-Trent would have been a major breakthrough, but was never built. The 5,000-square-metre building for Apple Computers (p. 44) at Stockley Park, a significant project for a prestige client, was realized (it was opened in 1989 after a fourteen-month construction period). The context was the classic new-style business park, where a team of architects (including Foster) worked within an Ove Arup Associates masterplan. The buildings were, in essence, pavilions in a park and Troughton McAslan's building (later extended in a second phase, with Troughton in charge) was distinctive, even decorative – fabric awnings were used to good effect externally for solar shading. The building was in the Foster–Rogers tradition, but its pragmatic character and rejection of the industrial look pointed the way beyond High-Tech. The central atrium is a genuinely usable and attractive communal space as well as a means of circulation. **John McAslan** was thirty-five when the first phase of the Apple building was completed and Jamie Troughton was thirty-nine. This was the age of '40 Under Forty' exhibitions, intended to showcase the talents of young architects and encourage developers to give them jobs. Some of these had huge largesse to distribute, none more so than Olympia & York,

Jamie Troughton (left) with John McAslan

Design House, London

St Peter's Street, London

Pierre Chareau's Maison de Verre, Paris

Glenn Murcutt's farmhouse, Australia

From initial experiments with modernism in the late 1980s, McAslan began to explore the roots of pioneering twentieth-century architecture by referring to precedents by Mendelsohn, Wright, Kahn, Piano and others, which resulted in a series of key projects by Troughton McAslan, such as Redhill station in 1990.

who were building Canary Wharf in London's Docklands. O&Y wanted big office buildings without delay – the 'Big Bang' of 1986, which deregulated the financial markets, created a lively demand for space – and went initially to architects with whom they had already worked in North America. The development was, however, criticized as an undigested import – hence the decision to commission some buildings from British practices. Troughton McAslan were interviewed for one of them in 1988. The result was Building FC3 (p. 64) at Canary Wharf, completed in 1992. This was a big building by any standard and until recently it has stood apart from the run of buildings in the development, spurning facile Postmodernist historicism in favour of a more sophisticated reading of precedent. McAslan has never been entirely happy with the project, which he carried out to a carefully prescribed brief very similar to that for the other Canary Wharf blocks. But the elegance of the final product, distinguished by a 'wrapped skin' in the tradition of Wright's Johnson Wax Company Administration building (Racine, Wisconsin, 1936-38) and William Lescaze's Philadelphia Savings Fund Society building (1926-31), justifies the process. **John McAslan's** passionate interest in architectural theory – he recalls 'dabbling in history' from his student days onwards – began to find expression in his architecture quite early on. His heroes included not only Wright and Kahn, along with Mackintosh and other architects of the Free Style, but equally engineers and 'constructors' such as Owen Williams and Jean Prouvé. Williams's Daily Express buildings, one of them in Glasgow, undoubtedly influenced the design of the Canary Wharf building. He looked beyond the Modern movement to the work of original British designers such as Charles Holden, famous for his London Underground stations of the 1930s. Appropriately, Troughton McAslan won the competition for a new Underground training centre in 1989, although nothing was ever built. The new buildings at Redhill station (1990; p. 122) derive clearly from the model of Holden's stations on the Piccadilly Line. **The work** of Erich Mendelsohn was a significant 'discovery'. 'He became a rich source for me,' says McAslan, whose involvement with the De La Warr Pavilion in Bexhill-on-Sea began in 1991 and looks set to continue well into the new millennium. The building is one of the few world-class Modern movement buildings in Britain. In conservative Bexhill, it was always a bold, even foolhardy, experiment. By the 1980s the pavilion was in poor physical condition – though listed Grade I – and its future was highly uncertain, until the stakes were raised by a voluntary trust, which pressed for a programme of restoration and renaissance. McAslan could not resist the challenge. **Repairing and** adapting historic, even iconic, buildings – including Wright's Florida Southern College (p. 92); The Roundhouse (Camden Town, p. 104), Isokon (Lawn Road) Flats (p. 134) and the Peter Jones store (p. 32) in London; and Mackintosh's Bassett-Lowke House in Northampton (p. 108) – thereafter became something of an office speciality. McAslan himself pursued it and involved several members of the office in the various projects. Jamie Troughton was supportive but sceptical – by the early 1990s the interests of the two partners were beginning to diverge. It was Troughton, for example, who won and managed commissions for two Jubilee Line stations. It was not until 1996, however, that the partnership came to an amicable conclusion and John McAslan & Partners (JMP) was born. **John McAslan's** career has been driven by a need for new challenges and a dread of becoming comfortable or complacent. On occasions personally reticent, McAslan has a clear idea of making his own way and has an awareness of the sheer hard work needed to realize his dreams. 'The studio needs to succeed on the basis of adaptability and a positive view of change,' he says. Balancing rehabilitation work with new buildings is, he believes, vital to the health of the practice. He has a fervent desire to be involved in everything that

Redhill station, Surrey

De La Warr Pavilion,
Bexhill-on-Sea

Frank Lloyd Wright's Florida Southern College

Judiciary, Seychelles

British High Commission, Nairobi

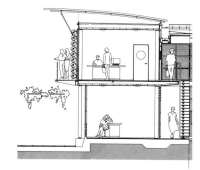

International commissions, which now form a significant element of the practice's work, began with the Nairobi High Commission and Seychelles Judiciary projects. The schemes experiment with low-energy contemporary interpretations of local building traditions, drawing on the work of Glenn Murcutt and Renzo Piano. St Catherine's College Institute in Kobe was the practice's first built project overseas.

the studio produces and, although he would like it slowly to evolve and grow, he does not intend to relinquish leadership. Other architects, he says, sadly appear to have 'often lost the plot' because they ceased to exercise this creative imprint and delegated to others, so that the key qualities of their work became diluted. For this reason, there is an expanding group of tried and trusted associates, including Murray Smith, Adam Brown, Andrew Hapgood, Roger Wu, Rachel Smart, Hiro Aso and Martin Markcrow, some of whom have spent most of their careers with him. **It was** McAslan who took the firm to distant places – Africa, the USA, Japan, Turkey and Italy, where he saw the opportunities to do the projects he wanted. Troughton McAslan's 1989 competition scheme for the new British High Commission in Nairobi was not successful (the project was awarded to Cullum & Nightingale instead) but was forward-looking in its marriage of traditional and modern technology and provision for future change. High commissions were traditionally places apart, aloof outposts of the mother culture. McAslan proposed a group of buildings that could be erected by local craftsmen and that were responsive to the local climate. The work of Renzo Piano and Glenn Murcutt – who designs buildings that 'sit light-ly on the land' – influenced the scheme. McAslan believes that its virtues lay in its simplicity and directness, qualities he seeks to achieve in all his buildings. Avoiding formalism and 'obvious gestures' is, he says, a prime concern of the work. **Japan was** a more daunting prospect even than Africa. When Nigel Coates and David Chipperfield were being fêted for their shops and bars in Tokyo, McAslan trumped them and built an entire college campus in Kobe. The St Catherine's College Institute (p. 82) at Kobe, completed in 1991, was (and is) unique, the result of an alliance between an Oxford college, whose building was designed by Arne Jacobsen (1959–64), and Japanese patronage aimed at importing British culture to Japan. Too little known in Britain, yet an

award-winning scheme in Japan, the Kobe campus is a bold gesture, drawing, not surprisingly, on Jacobsen's St Catherine's but equally on the tough aesthetic of Kahn. Ironically, there is nothing specifically British about the development. Only the clock tower, a conces-sion to nostalgia, which McAslan regretted at the time – 'we should have fought harder against it' – jars in a scheme that points the way to later projects. 'I felt that Kobe gave us the opportunity to be less cautious and more innovative than we were being in Britain,' he says. It is no accident that some of McAslan's most important jobs of the last few years, the product of the practice's maturity, lie outside Britain. **The search** for an alternative to High-Tech in the late 1980s had taken McAslan and his colleagues some way towards a for-malist approach – most apparent in the 1986 competition scheme for the Indira Gandhi Centre in New Delhi and in the modest but interest-ing (and certainly Italian-inspired) Alexander House, set in a banal south London shopping parade. Both projects are somewhat 'styled' and McAslan, who is unhappy with the idea of 'styling' buildings, does not regard them as particularly significant. He has never warmed to the Postmodernist agenda and its finite, designer-object products, but, like many essentially modern architects, has benefited from the breaking down of dogmatic attitudes to history and style. The apartment block close to the Thames at Rotherhithe (p. 134) is, in a sense, an act of homage to the 'white modern' style of the 1930s. The roughly contem-porary housing developments to either side of the block are a reminder, however, that virtually all docklands housing at the time was low-rise, brick-clad and neo-vernacular history, undigested and ill-understood. Getting consent for an elegant little apartment tower was quite an achievement, with which the support of the Royal Fine Art Commission and others helped. **A sense** of history and context is detectable in the work of most mainstream Western architects at the

Renzo Piano's Menil Art Museum, Houston

St Catherine's College Institute, Kobe

Frank Lloyd Wright's Johnson Wax building, Racine, Wisconsin

Button and Bilbow's Stockwell bus garage, London

Francisco Berenguer's chapel, Garrat, Spain

Industrial ruin, Gourock, Scotland

Louis Kahn's Dhakar Assembly Hall, Bangladesh

John McAslan's major recent and ongoing international projects include the Max Mara headquarters near Milan and the Yapi Kredi Bank operations centre south of Istanbul (Kahnian in inspiration) being exemplars.

end of the twentieth century. Piano's work exhibits a particularly powerful response, but projects such as Foster's Carré d'Art at Nîmes and Rogers's European law courts at Bordeaux demonstrate the degree to which these erstwhile High-Tech leaders have shifted their former positions. McAslan's Max Mara headquarters (p. 26), near Reggio Emilia, brings together a number of themes in his work, not least the perennial influence of Louis Kahn. Its sources are international but the complex of buildings draws strongly on McAslan's awareness of Italian traditions – he spends his summers in a house in Tuscany (p. 140). Like so many other Italian companies, Max Mara is proud of its roots. It is family-run, and McAslan and his colleagues worked intensively with the owners to develop a project that looks at home in the rich, agrarian landscape of the Po Valley, which has been intensively farmed since Roman times. The region's characteristic farm groups, generally arranged to a highly formal plan and framed by plantations of cypresses, strongly influenced McAslan's scheme, designed for flexibility and future growth. The landscape architect Peter Walker, who has become an occasional McAslan collaborator, was brought in at an early stage to develop a strategy for integrating the complex into its setting. As the site is close to the A1 *autostrada*, baffling the noise of traffic is one practical objective. The buildings form a 'family', clustered around 'streets'. The uses they house are various – offices, warehousing, showrooms and studios for designers – but there is no sense of hierarchy. This is a democratic, creative workplace for the twenty-first century. **Finding good** clients is satisfying for any architect. John McAslan seems to have assembled a richly atypical client list. Even when the client is a large institution, there is always a creative individual with whom the office has worked – such as Ian Caldwell, estates director at Imperial College, London, for which JMP completed a major extension to the library in 1997 (p. 76). Such projects as The Roundhouse (p. 104), powered by the philan-

thropist Torquil Norman, and the Bexhill Pavilion (p. 98), where local councillor Jill Theis was the catalyst for the regeneration scheme, are natural McAslan territory. Arts buildings look set to remain a prominent feature of the JMP workload. The masterplan for the Royal Academy of Music (p. 88), close to Regent's Park, shows the firm on top form, devising a strategy for the Academy to remain on its historic site and yet to expand and develop high-quality facilities for the future. Given the scale and variety of the projects it has in hand, it is surprising to discover that the McAslan studio consists of no more than thirty people and yet is able to compete confidently with far larger practices. **Jamie Troughton** was instrumental in securing the commission for the Yapi Kredi operations centre (p. 18), outside Istanbul. McAslan, having developed a dynamic working relationship with Yapi Kredi's president, Burhan Karacam, brought the scheme to fruition. He sees this as a landmark in his career: it was a foundation of the new practice and is close to his heart on a number of counts. 'I said to myself: I must do this on my own,' McAslan recalls. 'So I seized the moment.' The basic format of the Yapi Kredi project has affinities with the Max Mara headquarters and is basically Kahnian – a series of independent buildings linked by streets (in this case, internal and comfort-cooled to cope with the extremes of the Turkish climate, but perhaps also in the style of traditional Turkish markets). Peter Walker was again brought in to devise a landscape concept for the exposed site. The complex honours, with modesty, certain traditional responses that are rooted in Ottoman architecture, without ever being condescending. There are no explicit 'Islamic' references: the buildings are international, rugged, made for hard wear and long life. In such a recent project (designed and built between 1994 and 1998) it is surprising, perhaps, to find strong echoes of High-Tech rhetoric – notably the dialogue between the fair-faced concrete frame and the extensive use of glass

Italian landscape

Max Mara headquarters, Reggio Emilia

YKB operations centre, Istanbul

Louis Kahn's Richards Medical
Laboratory, Philadelphia

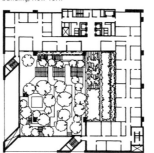

Kevin Roche's Ford Foundation
building, New York

and metal inside the building. But this is High-Tech for its time, achieved on a carefully controlled budget and to a strict schedule, using state-of-the-art, low-energy technology. **The Yapi Kredi** headquarters building (p. 38), designed for a site in central Istanbul, is more clearly a prestige project. By London or New York standards, the building is modest in scale but it promises to be a beautifully crafted showpiece. It is a sophisticated exercise in Modernist historicism, its strong echoes of Kevin Roche's Ford Foundation acting as a reminder of McAslan's American affiliations. The inclusion of a generous public 'square', a cultural facility where part of the bank's extensive art collection will be shown, reinforces the transatlantic character of the building. McAslan is unapologetic about the American influences in his work – he admires the adaptability and initiative of a number of American practices while regretting the degree to which they have too often drifted from their Modernist roots. No present-day architect, certainly no American, has studied and drawn upon the work of Louis Kahn with McAslan's skill and intelligence. The little school for hearing-impaired children at Christopher Place, close to Euston Station, London (p. 70), is an adept and sophisticated essay in space, materials and light, which could have been designed only by someone who reveres the Mellon Center at Yale. **McAslan has** had the good fortune to complete a number of substantial new buildings and there are more in the pipeline – an office building in Queen Victoria Street in the City of London, a new music school in the shell of the King Charles Building at Greenwich, a scheduled ancient monument for Trinity College of Music, a new gallery of modern art in Middlesbrough, a healthcare facility in Kent, an office building by Soho Square, for example. He has the ability and the drive – which he instils also into his colleagues – to grasp the issues behind a client brief, to draw up an initial proposal very quickly, then to work with the client to develop it. The elegant and practical

lantern in the lecture room at the Royal Society of Arts in London, a listed building that was basically being refurbished, with limited scope for innovative new design, is an instance of the care that goes into projects of this kind. McAslan says that working with buildings by such masters as Wright, Mendelsohn, Kahn (McAslan has made a study of his Bath House at Trenton, New Jersey) and Wells Coates is neither a diversion nor a prestige lossleader: understanding how these great precursors worked is an education for a present-day practitioner. 'The range of our jobs is important for morale,' he insists. **Architects worldwide** are increasingly working with existing buildings, whether masterworks or merely valuable resources that are too good to squander. For McAslan, this field has added a substantial theoretical element to the work of the office. It is McAslan's ability to reconfigure and regenerate old buildings, rather than simply to repair historic buildings, that is one of the prime strengths of his practice. McAslan is not primarily a theorist but he has strong views on the way that the urban fabric can be made to work. **His approach** to such work has developed from a study of practice in Europe and America. He finds the typically British approach – piecemeal repair and addition – unsatisfactory and advocates a full audit of a building's fabric, failings and potential, as is general in the USA, as the first step towards renewal. London's King's Cross station, where McAslan is working on a development masterplan for Railtrack (p. 130), is large even by late twentieth-century standards and is more intensively used than at any time in its 150 years of existence. Listed Grade I, the station has been extensively altered over the years and is currently prefaced by a 1970s concourse whose flimsiness and shoddiness insult the great brick, iron and timber sheds behind. (There is a reference to the old King's Cross in the concert hall McAslan has designed for the Royal Academy of Music, a kilometre away along the Euston Road.) It is possible that adapting King's

YKB's operations centre commission led to the practice's design for its headquarters in downtown Istanbul (note the latter's debt to Kevin Roche's Ford Foundation building in New York). It promises to be a significant landmark, as do the buildings the firm is designing in central London for the School of Oriental and African Studies.

SOAS, London

Yapi Kredi Bank headquarters, Istanbul

Pierre Chareau's Robert
Motherwell Studio, Long Island

The Roundhouse, London

Royal Academy of Music, London

Cross for its future role may at the same time permit a return to its historic format. JMP's work at Paddington station in connection with the Heathrow Express rail link shows what can be achieved. **Strict preservation** may be appropriate for medieval churches and Tudor cottages, but it is unlikely to guarantee the survival of large nineteenth- and twentieth-century buildings that have to adapt to changing needs. Equally, 'embalming' buildings means that the process of transformation, practised from the age of Andrea Palladio to that of Carlo Scarpa, is permanently vetoed. The problem is acute in Britain – where a transformation as radical as, say, that achieved by Jean Nouvel at the Lyons opera house, would be unlikely to gain consent. McAslan's major reconstruction project for the listed Peter Jones store in London (p. 32) – a thoroughly modern building that has been consistently popular since it opened in 1936 – takes account of these issues. It identifies the key features of the building that are sacrosanct (chiefly the exterior), proposes a strategy for making it operationally and commercially more effective and dares to insert new elements in keeping with the original. The proposed full-height atrium, with escalators snaking upwards, promises to give London what it has previously lacked – a store interior with something of the thrill and panache of the best of Paris and Chicago. **McAslan is**, indeed, a key figure – maybe *the* key figure – in the development of a more creative and innovative approach to adaptation and renovation in Britain. It is a difficult game to play, he concedes, since the goalposts keep moving. A commission from London University's School of Oriental and African Studies (SOAS) to extend its complex in Bloomsbury (p. 96) meant not only dealing with an existing listed building (by Holden, though a late and low-key effort) but also with another, potentially 'listable' building by Sir Denys Lasdun, one of the most respected of senior British practi-

tioners and, in his mid-eighties, well able to fight for the integrity of his work. **McAslan's task** was therefore one of negotiation and dialogue – with Lasdun, local residents, English Heritage and amenity bodies, as well as with the client – to achieve an acceptable strategy. Lasdun's work is tough and intractable, critically admired if not highly popular. McAslan admires its toughness and directness. The resulting scheme has met with approval and yet promises to have an integrity of its own. **Architecture, like** all the arts, needs to push forward to guarantee its vitality. It is also rooted in history, precedent and experience – today's architects revisit the work of Alvar Aalto, Le Corbusier, Kahn, Wright and others as their predecessors did that of Andrea Palladio and Leon Battista Alberti. The Modern movement pioneers deluded themselves when they decreed an architecture free of precedent, devoid of history, detached from the past. John McAslan is certainly a 'pragmatic' architect – no bad thing – but he is also an idealist. A concern for continuity and integrity, which underlies his near-obsession with quality, is balanced by an expansive urge to experiment, to push things to the limit. McAslan's work is perhaps most remarkable for the fertile way in which it accommodates history, with respect but without overdue reverence, treating history as a living tradition, not a static quantity. It is this quality permeating his work that makes it unique among British architects of his generation. McAslan is an individualist, his attitudes forged in his youth, but he is also part of a great tradition.

BUILDINGS

Yapi Kredi Bank operations centre

Turkey's Yapi Kredi Bank is the client for two major buildings by McAslan, part of a 'family' of recent projects by the practice, all of them large, international and designed for the needs of major organizations. (Four schemes accounted for some £150 million worth of construction work.) The 46,000-square-metre operations centre located some 50 km south east of Istanbul is, superficially at least, an international product that pays no special regard to the local vernacular. Its antecedents are various, but the work of Louis Kahn is evoked, along with the diagrams of Henning Larsen's Trondheim University and Niels Torp's SAS headquarters. There are also memories of Herman Hertzberger's pioneering approach to workplace design. The plan does, however, have a regional resonance in its references to the covered markets and arcades of old Istanbul, a format surprisingly relevant to the new, interactive office. Flexibility and the potential to accommodate future growth were prime features of the client brief – at present, the complex houses 1,800 staff. The molecular plan, with structurally independent blocks linked by internal 'streets' (glazed or fabric-covered), is a response to these requirements. Hardly had work started on site than Yapi Kredi asked for two additional blocks to be added to the original eight. There were no practical problems in expanding the programme, such was the adaptability of the design diagram. The East/West dialogue that underlies the scheme is also expressed in the servicing strategy, which is essentially low-energy, using natural ventilation and solar control to confront Turkey's humid summers and icy winters. A landscape scheme, which 'reforests' the site, by McAslan's favoured collaborator, Peter Walker, completes a progressive but pragmatic ensemble, which combines economy with high-quality finishes and some striking internal spaces. The complex carries echoes of hilltop settlements throughout history, whether military, domestic or religious in purpose. A little raw at first, as all such places are, it is developing as an acropolis, melding with the landscape while bleaching gradually in the sun. Perhaps the greatest compliment Yapi Kredi pays to its host country, however, is not to be condescending. The design does not pilfer local motifs or assume a fake vernacular or a needless grandiosity. Instead, it honours, with modesty, certain traditional responses to conditions in that part of the world, which the modern architect would be wise to learn. The house of the family of Yapi Kredi is a harmonious one.

Diagrammatic plan of the project

Tower construction

Top-floor landing

Early-morning view

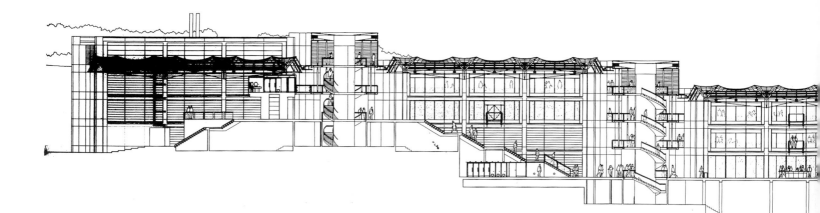

Cross section through the complex, access bridges and gorge

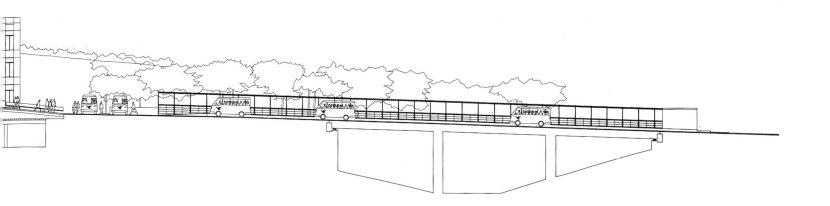

Internal street and tower views

Street café atrium

External and internal street views

Max Mara headquarters The project was won by JMP in competition in 1995 and is another of the international projects that have underpinned the practice's success in the 1990s. The client is typically Italian, both in its dynamism on the international fashion scene and in its attachment to its roots in the Po Valley. There was a clear desire to create a memorable development, which had a clear relationship to the context of flat fields, long poplar avenues and big skies and was at home in an agrarian landscape. Working with landscape architect Peter Walker, McAslan developed a strategy for integrating buildings and landscape, with regular tree planting defining the site and forming a setting for buildings that are, in their undemonstrative dignity, in tune with the traditional architecture of the region. As with the Yapi Kredi Bank operations centre, the plan is molecular, Kahnian, made for flexibility and growth and for good working conditions – although at Max Mara, the linking 'streets' are external rather than covered. The plan reflects the interlinked operations of Max Mara's constituent companies and provides for a mix of offices, showrooms and warehousing on a site close to the *autostrada*. The exceptionally clear diagram of this architecture/landscape scheme commands respect even in a country where modern ideals of planning were first developed. Like Palladio's villa complexes, the headquarters are really a city in miniature.

Site model showing energy centre, car park,
forest glade, offices and showroom

Perimeter detail of offices

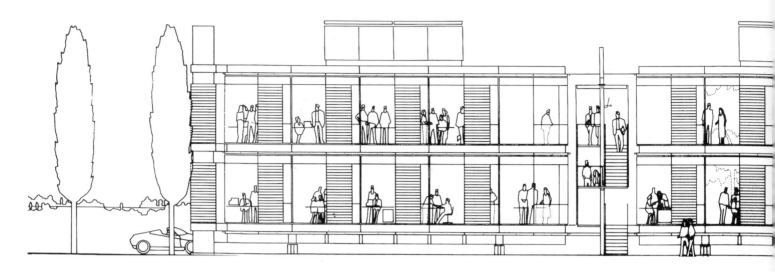

Offices elevation

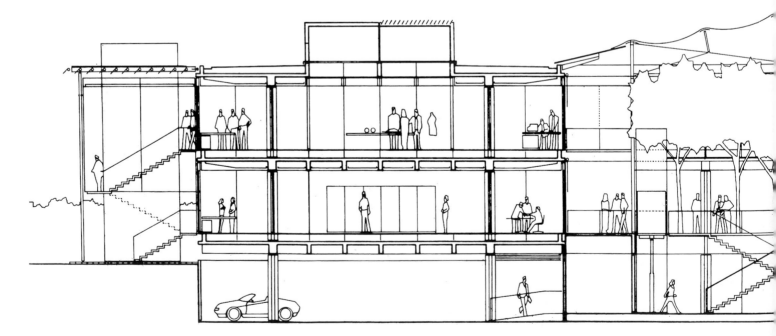

Offices cross section

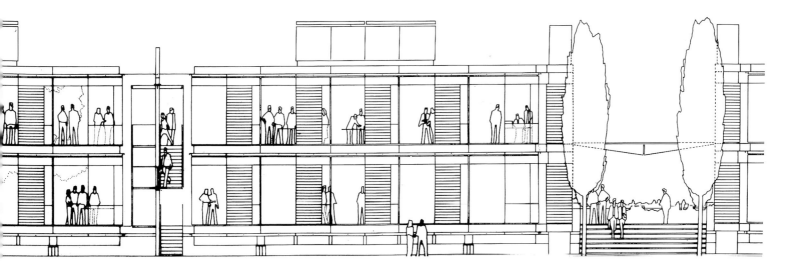

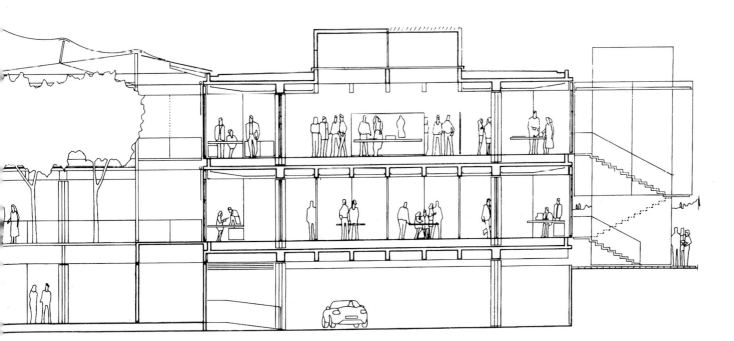

[Overleaf] Offices study models

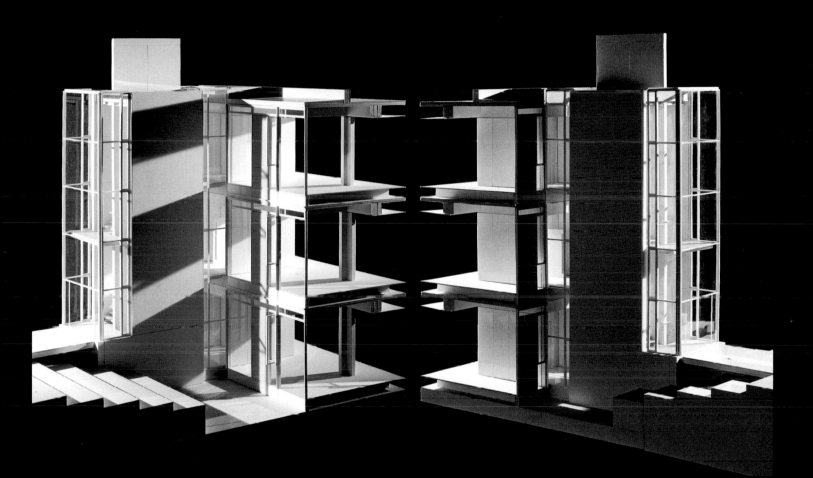

Peter Jones   Located in Chelsea, the building is a London landmark. Although derivative of the much-published German store designs of Erich Mendelsohn, the building (by Slater & Moberly, 1935-37) is a Modern movement classic (listed Grade II*), elegantly turning the corner into the King's Road from Sloane Square. Commonly assumed to be all of one piece, the store was, in fact, built in phases – the last as late as the 1960s. The Second World War halted work and spared the last part of the old Peter Jones store, together with a fine 1890s house by A H Mackmurdo, now incorporated into the store. The interiors are, on the whole, disappointing and, in places, cramped and inconvenient, a consequence of the extended building programme. JMP was called in to rationalize and update the building to give it a new lease of life for the twenty-first century, installing modern services, improving access and storage facilities and making the upper floors more accessible and inviting to shoppers. The brief was unashamedly commercial, recognizing that this is first and foremost a shop, but also showed an awareness of the landmark value of the building. Externally, there will be only minimal changes. Inside, however, a spectacular new atrium will be created (also acting as a plenum system for extracting air and smoke) with escalator access throughout the building. Staff and shoppers will benefit from modern ventilation, better lighting and the elimination of untidy level changes on upper floors. This is a model scheme of practical conservation.

Original building perspective, 1935

Peter Jones under construction, 1937

Peter Jones, existing views

[Overleaf] Study model of proposed remodelling

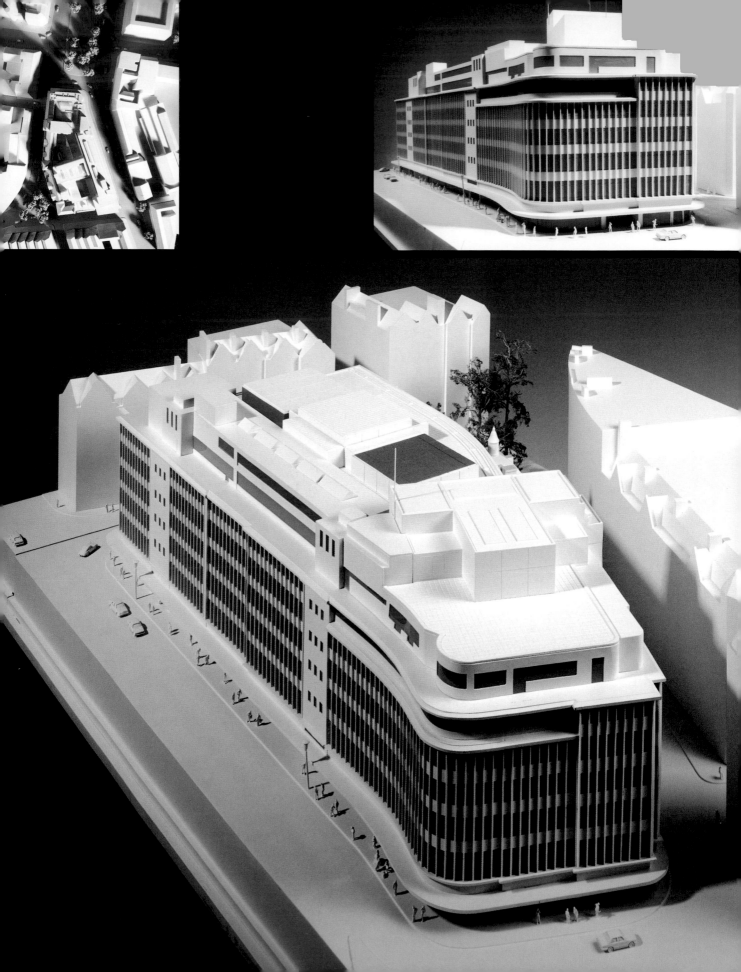

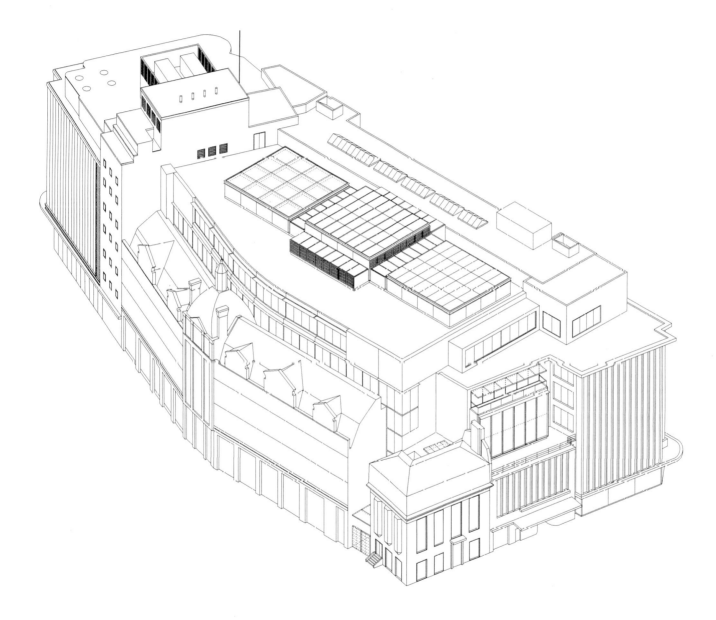

Aerial view of roof extensions

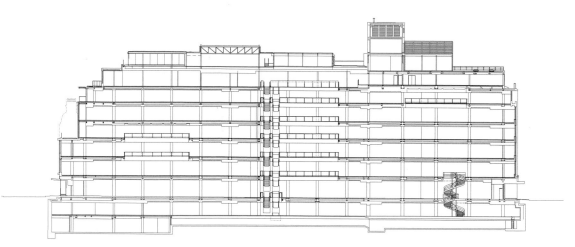

Cross sections showing roof extensions and extended light well

Operational models of proposed roof extensions
(above) and existing organization (below)

Yapi Kredi Bank headquarters No more than a third the size of the operations centre, The Yapi Kredi headquarters building in central Istanbul is a consciously 'prestige' scheme, with a clear image-making role alongside its functional programme. The inspirations behind McAslan's designs are international and, to a degree, American – Kevin Roche's Ford Foundation was an obvious influence. This is a city building, designed to be on public view. As in the Ford building, the atrium has a semi-public life and is intended to display items from the bank's extensive art collection. The remainder of the building contains executive offices and general administration and trading floors, with extensive secure areas at basement level. The low-energy approach adopted at the operations centre is also pursued here in the traffic-torn centre of the city. A zone of intensive planting, set within the building's perimeter 'buffer' zone, is part of the energy strategy. This is a landmark building of great elegance, which, for all its modest scale, would be equally at home in Manhattan or the City of London.

Study models

Study model

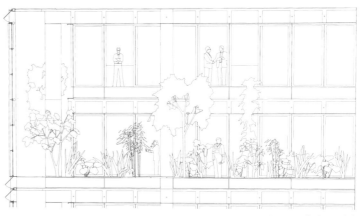

Perimeter 'buffer' zone study

Cross section through the proposed headquarters, with courtyard
garden and pavilion on the left

Commerce

Queen Victoria Street   This project – which will be McAslan's first completed building in the City of London – occupies a site that has been occupied by the Salvation Army since 1881. The Army's original block was destroyed in the Blitz and an undistinguished building was erected on the site in 1963. McAslan replaces this with a striking new design in steel and glass, the form of which derives from its sensitive location close to St Paul's Cathedral. The key organizational principle is the use of full-height internal streets that extend north–south throughout the building, in a reference to the lost historic street pattern that extended from St Paul's to the river. The result is that the building reads as a series of linked pavilions. The site is, fortuitously, on an important future route – from the Cathedral to the new Bankside Tate, via the Millennium Footbridge, which the new building's west flank will adjoin.

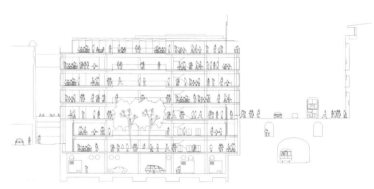

Cross section

Study context model, with St Paul's Cathedral visible

Apple Computers headquarters

The Apple building was the first major new-build project completed by the Troughton McAslan office. It was a landmark for the practice – an entirely new building for a prestige user on a greenfield site, a contrast to the series of modest-cost rehabs it had previously undertaken. Stockley Park, near Heathrow, remains the classic 1980s business park, with buildings by many notable practices in a landscaped setting created out of a former refuse tip. Completed in 1989, Phase I of the Apple development is an assured performance for a young practice. Superficially, the building is a 'pavilion in the park', but the plan, around an internal street, is innovative and practical. The building is made more distinctive by the use of graceful tensile sunshades, which relieve the regularity of the Miesian grid. A second phase of the scheme was completed in 1991, doubling the size of the development but allowing both buildings to be used independently if necessary.

Detail of external façade

Internal street

External detail

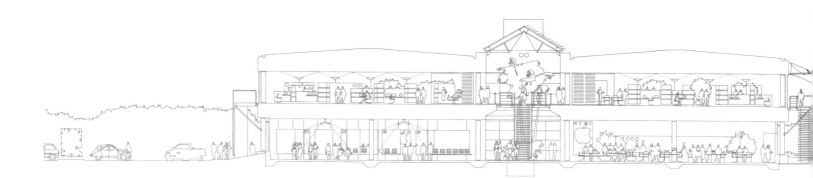

Cross section

Thames & Hudson Offices   The prestigious international art and architecture publisher Thames & Hudson Ltd operated for decades from a group of interconnected Georgian houses close to the British Museum, an appropriate and appealing home but one that grew increasingly overcrowded and inconvenient for its 120 employees. In connection with the company's fiftieth anniversary, an extensive search was launched to find premises that would signal a fresh change and provide a revitalized new working environment. Esavian House, a tough 1930s warehouse in High Holborn originally used for educational supplies, was selected for its full servicing provision (from a central core), a vital component for the company's latest digital technology and information systems, and its dramatic double-height reception area, which suggested a space reminiscent of Pierre Chareau's Maison de Verre in Paris and could house part of the firm's extensive library. Many of the building's features were left intact as the top three levels were opened up to maximize natural light, communication, interdepartmental interaction and openness. The open-plan conversion was ideally suited to McAslan's brand of pragmatic, highly detailed work, and there are numerous elements of delight: the fine maple surfaces that combine elegantly with the glassed-in offices, a glazed staircase whose transparency is delicately layered through the offices' countless floor-to-ceiling glass walls and the user-friendly coffee bar/kitchen areas on each floor.

Exterior views of the reception at night

Interior view

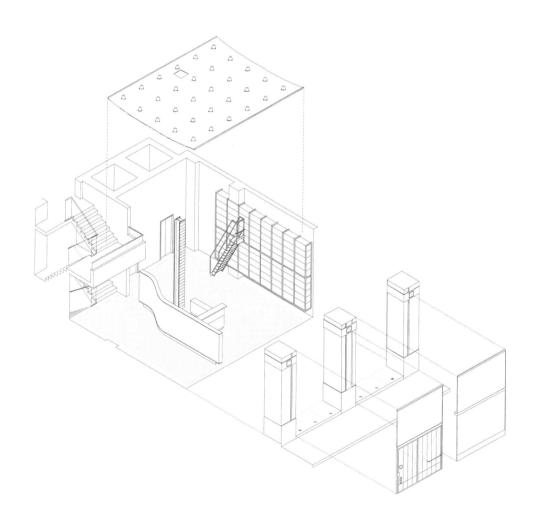

Exploded axonometric of reception

Stair and office details

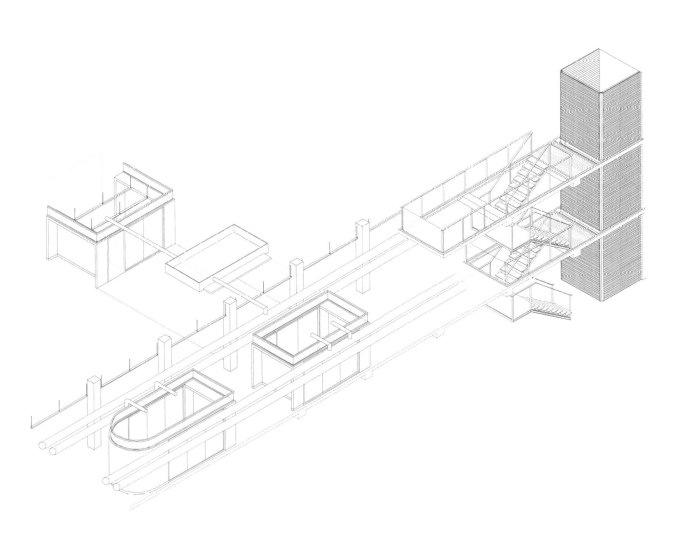

Exploded axonometric of office level

Colebrooke Place Completed in 1990, 1–3 Colebrooke Place is perhaps the most striking example of McAslan's ability to make something not only useful but also attractive out of a very unpromising structure. The starting point was a building that, in conventional terms, would not count as architecture: a basic, rather dilapidated shed, dating from the 1950s, structurally sound but otherwise utterly unremarkable. It was turned into an inspiring workplace by apparently simple means: the careful use of natural light, repairs to original finishes and the insertion of a mezzanine level along one side of the interior space. The mezzanine is carried on beautifully formed concrete columns. It is the attention to materials that transforms the building – brickwork was simply painted and oak floors cleaned and sealed. The interventions are straightforward, with no superfluous detailing. The rehabilitation cost a mere £400,000.

Studio

Reception

Interior details

Gallery

St Peter's Street   One of the earliest refurbishment schemes carried out by McAslan and his former partner, Jamie Troughton, St Peter's Street set a standard for low-cost rehabilitations that was rarely matched. The raw material was a Victorian warehouse, which was the subject of a straightforward two-phase scheme, launched in 1988 and completed in 1991, to convert it into the studios of an advertising agency. The aim was to retain the original structure, wherever possible, in an uncompromised form. Cabling and other services were left exposed but every new element was carefully detailed. The new work centres round a double-height entrance space, which echoes the court outside and allows light into the depths of the interior. The entrance space contains an exceptionally elegant new staircase and is mediated with the courtyard outside by the old façade. The reconfigured façade consists of a window, a door, a beam and a downpipe, which neatly express the organization of the interior while simply stating the elementary qualities of a building: structure, enclosure, the admission of light. A wall of glass bricks – another reference to the Maison de Verre – is a practical as well as aesthetic device.

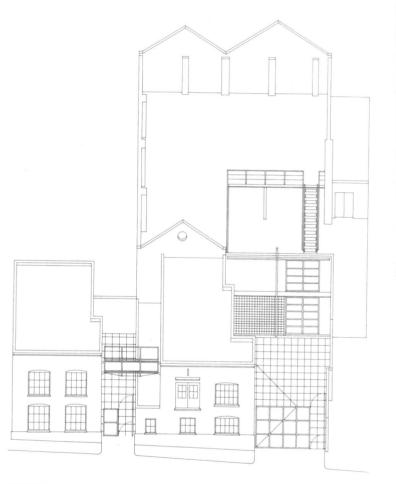

Axonometric of proposals

Rosebery Avenue and Hardwick Street   Completed in 1992, this scheme epitomizes the essential philosophy of the McAslan office. First, it combines the refurbishment of a sound 1920s industrial block with the construction of a new office building, to house both office and design studio accommodation. Part of the original building was, however, demolished to allow the construction of the new block, which faces on to Rosebery Avenue and features an exceptionally well-proportioned and detailed glazed façade in the tradition of Mies. Second, there was a willingness to adapt the old structure boldly to new practical needs, including the need for up-to-date servicing. Circulation and services are concentrated in a new glazed link carved out between the two retained blocks. The completed complex is characterized by the contrast between old and new and between historic and modern materials. The interest in materials and attention to detail is again typical of McAslan.

The building as found

Exterior detail of Rosebery Avenue

Hardwick Street link/brick bridge and stairs

External detail of Hardwick Street

Commerce

25 The North Colonnade, Canary Wharf

Winning the commission for a 37,000-square-metre block at Canary Wharf – the first British practice to build there – was a remarkable achievement, although the building's context was an essentially North American Beaux Arts masterplan. In contrast, McAslan's sixteen-storey building is defiantly modern in its aesthetic, declining to hide its high-performance specification under a Postmodern Classical skin. The inspirations are, indeed, clearly those of the Modern movement and the smooth and curvaceous glazed elevations owe a good deal to Wright's Johnson Wax building and to the buildings designed by engineer Owen Williams for the *Daily Express*. The building has a timeless dignity, which, as the new century dawns, sets it apart from its triumphantly (and now dated) 1980s neighbours and links it to the newer buildings at Canary Wharf, including the two towers designed by Norman Foster. In this project, McAslan proved that it was possible to work in a corporate framework, in line with a tight technical and constructional brief (and with associate architects) and yet achieve something distinctive and, in its way, classic.

25 The North Colonnade (bottom right) under construction

25 The North Colonnade (centre) in context

Shepherd's Bush Studios

A low-cost but stylish remake of a matter-of-fact old building for the new service industries that were reshaping the economy of Margaret Thatcher's London, the studios for a design company were created within the shell of a three-storey, concrete-framed warehouse. The architects' task was twofold: to solve the functional problem of organizing space and services and to devise an imagery appropriate to the new use. The interior of the building was reorganized around a new, triple-height, top-lit space, boldly carved out of the old structure and providing a focus for circulation and interaction. The services are exposed and even celebrated in the High-Tech manner, to almost sculptural effect. Robustness is balanced by delicacy, in the form of the new staircases and purpose-made furniture and lighting fixtures.

Uplighter

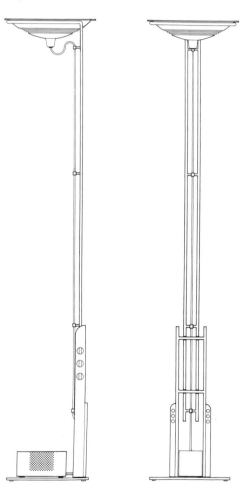

Conference rooms and atrium

Atrium and bridge

Design House   The property boom of the 1980s produced big new office buildings in London's City and Docklands, but there was equally a demand for a new sort of space to house the many small businesses that blossomed – architects, designers and public relations and advertising firms. Relaxation of planning regulations blurred the formerly rigid divide between office and industrial uses. The 'B1' space was one of the distinctive building types of the time in Britain, generally housed in refurbished factories and warehouses that had become redundant because of the decline of older industries. Design House, Troughton McAslan's first project, was created in 1984 out of a former car showroom, a solid but otherwise unremarkable 1950s structure. The scheme was essentially low-cost. The stripping back of the existing structure and the insertion of a mezzanine into the double-height space, with cellular offices below, created a light and flexible interior, with new services frankly exposed. The sharply detailed new façade gives the building a distinctive identity on its prominent corner site in Camden Town, which remains as fresh today as it was when completed in 1984.

Top-lit mezzanine studio

Entrance detail

Christopher Place

JMP was initially commissioned to develop an office building in this quiet mews close to Euston station. The office scheme was a victim of the 1990s recession and the site was donated by the developer to a charity that wished to build the UK's first centre of its kind catering for hearing-impaired children. McAslan worked with the new clients, notably the dynamic director, Angela Harding, to develop the Speech, Language and Hearing Centre, which opened in 1996. Christopher Place is a small gem of a building, with a clear infusion of the influence of Louis Kahn. It is rigorously disciplined and quietly monumental, yet the interiors are welcoming and child-scaled, with provision for the special needs of the users. Judicious use and the honest expression of good, natural materials, including slate and timber, give the building the look of quality - all to a tight budget.

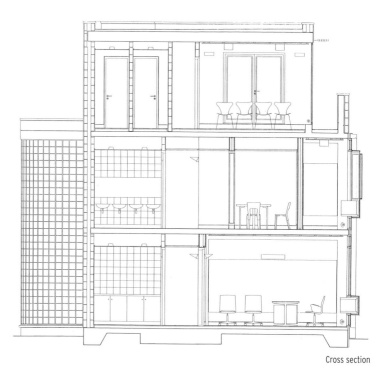

Cross section

Precedent: Louis Kahn's Esherick house, 1959-61

Entrance volume

Interior details of reception and audiology room

Parents' room

Reception alcove

Rear elevation

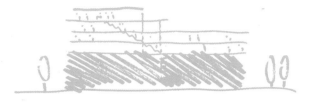

Imperial College Libraries   One of the world's leading centres of scientific research and education, Imperial College occupies a densely built-up site in the museums quarter of South Kensington ('Alberto-polis') and has developed rapidly since the Second World War. Most of its postwar (largely 1960s) buildings are of no great distinction and the library, designed originally by Norman & Dawbarn, is no exception. But it overlooks the Queen's Lawn, the college's most important green space, with the lofty tower of the old Imperial Institute – the rest was torn down in the 1960s – as its centrepiece. The library block was engineered for future expansion and there were no structural problems in adding two new floors on top. The issues were those of aesthetics, practical performance and value for money. A prime requirement was that the library remain open throughout the building works, with only a few short closed periods during vacations. The new steel-framed structure sits on the 1960s concrete grid. It is characterized by lightness – McAslan cites the work of Craig Ellwood as an exemplar. The 1960s building is vertical in emphasis, with tall, slit-like window openings. The addition is fully glazed, with fritted glass used to provide solar control and very slender framing. Comfort cooling was introduced to provide agreeable working conditions. There was little money for trimmings, but a new entrance lobby and bookshop provide a decent prelude to the new reading spaces. The library extension, completed in 1997, was Phase I of JMP's project to refurbish 1960s buildings on the site, in line with an overall masterplan. This is a direct response, yet it has produced something of genuine elegance out of unpromising raw material.

Construction detail

Elevational transparency at night

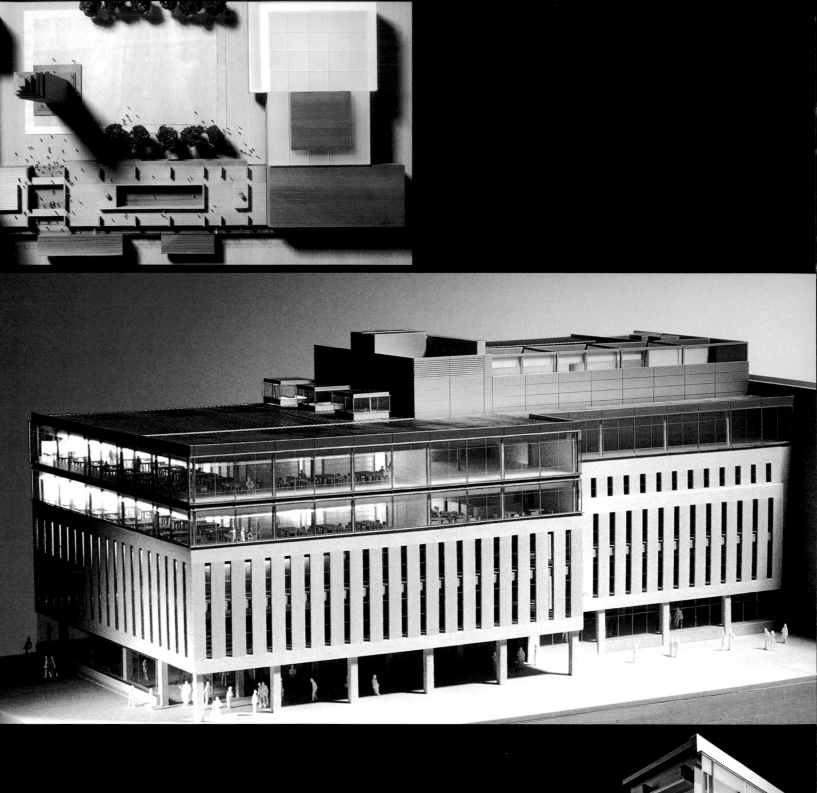
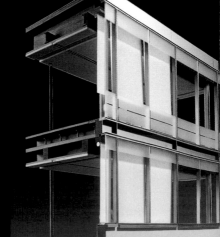

External detail

[From top] Models of the site, roof extension and façade

Education

Interior views

St Catherine's College Institute

The completion in 1991 of St Catherine's College Institute – linked to St Catherine's, Oxford – was a landmark for McAslan. Few British architects have completed substantial buildings in Japan and even Norman Foster and Richard Rogers have built on only a limited scale. Working in Japan means working with the Japanese system of procurement and with Japanese contractors and consultants (although the engineer was Ove Arup & Partners). In effect, this was a design-and-construct project, albeit within a construction industry that achieves high quality through this approach, and with Takenaka as constructor, possibly Japan's most respected contractor. The buildings occupy a striking site overlooking the ocean and the designs use that location to good effect. McAslan resisted the temptation to produce a parody of Arne Jacobsen's St Catherine's or, indeed, to design in a consciously 'Oxbridge' manner (even if the clock-tower is a gesture in that direction). His buildings at Kobe are more American than English in inspiration, solid and with a dignity appropriate to their public role. Some existing structures had to be incorporated in the scheme, its fast-track schedule modelled on the methodology of the commercial sector. There was little scope for rethinking or for revisions. In lesser hands, the result could have been a scheme destined to be quietly forgotten, or even an acute embarrassment. Yet the Kobe buildings are handsome and memorable, with careful detailing. The scheme led McAslan and his team forward, opening the way for other foreign commissions (for example, in Turkey) and demonstrating their ability to cope with a difficult and unusual working environment.

Model with lecture hall (left) and main building (beyond); the central courtyard and residential pavilions (right)

Main entrance to the principal building

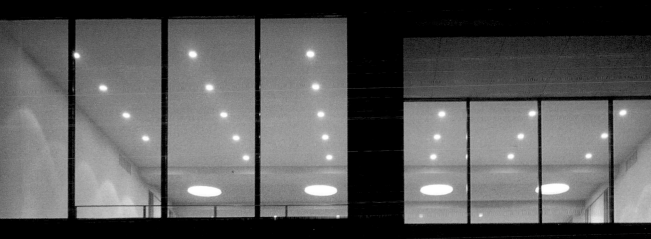

Lecture hall (left), central courtyard and residential pavilions (right)

Linked residential pavilions with barrel roof under construction

Linked residential pavilions seen from the park beneath

Internal and external details

Royal Academy of Music   The Heritage Lottery-funded scheme for the development of the world-famous Royal Academy of Music exemplifies the strengths of McAslan. The original building was completed in 1911 (by Ernest George, in a rather overblown Queen Anne manner) but the Academy has long outgrown it – in piecemeal fashion. McAslan's task was to masterplan a small campus, including the George building (to be remodelled and refurbished), the Nash terrace on York Gate (actually a postwar rebuild behind its stuccoed façade, which was to be extensively adapted to accommodate teaching and practice rooms as well as a 'living museum' of instruments) and new spaces to be created at basement level. In heritage-conscious London, it helps if new work can be kept out of sight. However, McAslan's new design on the campus, the concert hall, will be expressed externally as a glass-enclosed vaulted pavilion set between the existing buildings. This will be a strong, if discreet, product for the twenty-first century, somewhat inspired by Chareau's Long Island studio for Robert Motherwell. The scheme is due for completion in 2001.

York Gate being reconstructed, 1964

Recital pavilion in context

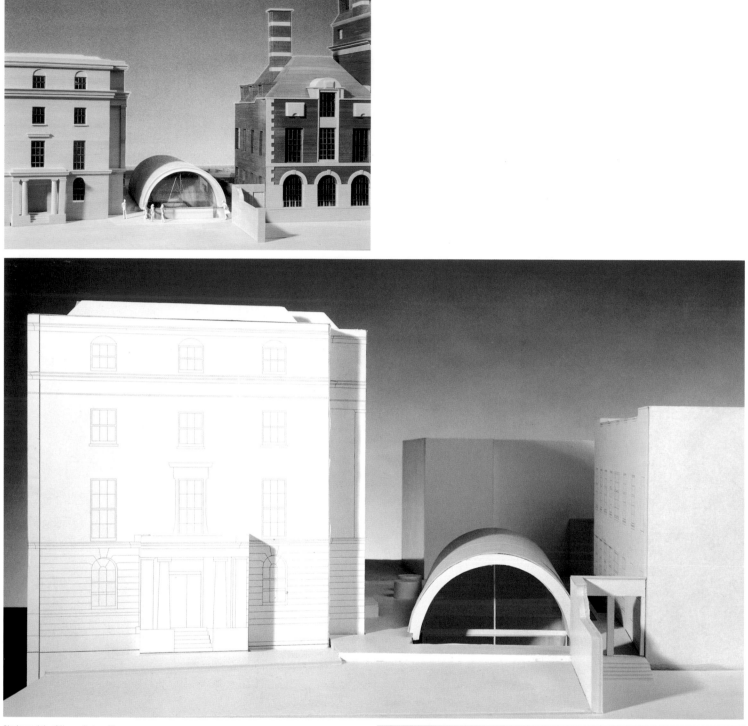

Study models of the recital pavilion

Early 'funnel' form of the recital pavilion

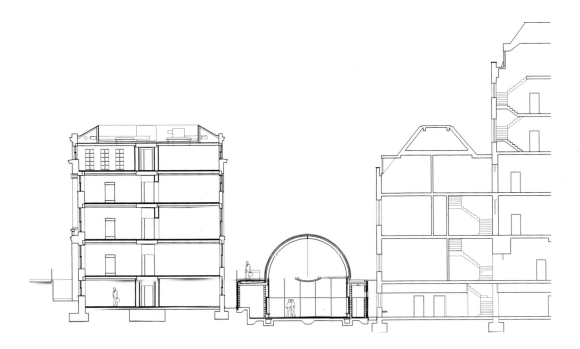

Cross section through York Gate, recital pavilion and Academy

Section through the recital pavilion, with York Gate beyond

Florida Southern College   JMP's extraordinary ability to adapt to the practical (and cultural) demands of overseas commissions and John McAslan's own admiration for the work of Frank Lloyd Wright are both reflected in the ongoing project to restore and refurbish the landmark campus at FSC. This is a late Wright work (built 1938–58), containing the greatest concentration of the master's work anywhere. The story of Wright's involvement is extraordinary in itself – he was brought in by the ambitious principal, Ludd Spivey, who involved many of the students in a self-build operation to create the campus. There are long-standing problems of repair and maintenance, which are at least partly attributable to the construction history. The buildings also lack modern services, including the air-conditioning that is standard equipment in steamy Florida. McAslan's work at FSC, beginning in 1993, was initially a matter of research and analysis, with John Figg of Ove Arup & Partners as technical collaborator. A strategy for repairing the existing buildings and for future growth was produced. McAslan finds the American approach to the repair of historic buildings, with its stress on embracing change and prolonging effective life and performance, more congenial than the preservation-oriented outlook prevalent in Britain. The $8-million remodelling of the 1958 Polk County Science Building, with Arup's New York office as engineer and Earl Walls of San Diego as laboratory planner, provides bold interventions to reuse this redundant teaching facility. The phased work is due for completion by 2001.

Detail of typical blockwork decay

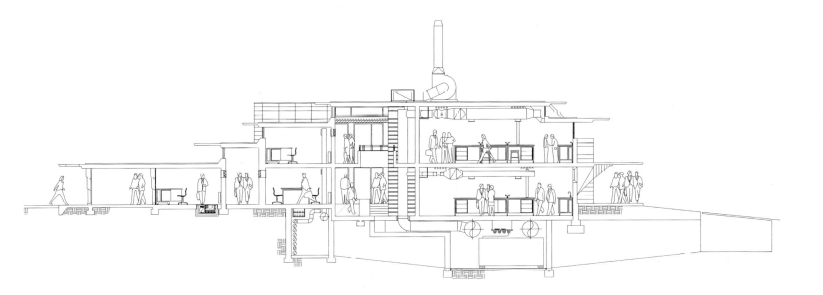

Proposed cross section through laboratories, service areas and support

Cross-sectional study model

School of Oriental and African Studies   Located on London University's central site in Bloomsbury, SOAS's original building is a rather ordinary listed late work of Charles Holden, a muted echo of his splendid Senate House nearby. A major extension, including a new library, was completed by Denys Lasdun in 1973 and is a significant work by a modern master. McAslan's project to extend SOAS, which began as a campus development plan in 1997, is rooted in respect for the work of Holden and Lasdun – the latter was consulted before proposals were drawn up. The principal area for growth is a narrow slice of land overlooking Torrington Square (which was mostly demolished by Holden before the Second World War). A heavily glazed new building, modularized to respond to Lasdun's building, will overlook the gardens, long neglected but due for upgrading as a focus for the university quarter. A smaller new block will be slotted in behind the Holden building. Neither of the original buildings will be significantly altered but lightly 'touched' to form atria and linkages. The project is a delicate exercise in responding to a complex urban setting, as well as to creative space management, low-energy servicing strategies and heritage politics.

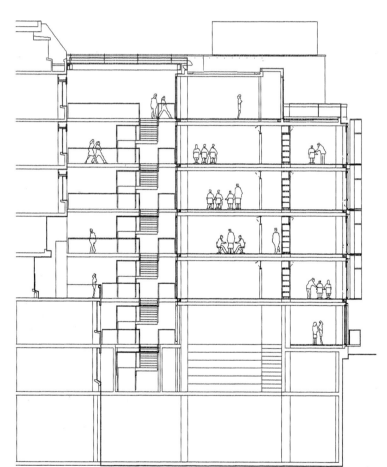

Cross section through proposed west wing, atrium and existing library

Study model of the west wing, with existing library beyond

The auditorium's steel frame under construction, 1934

De La Warr Pavilion McAslan's professional involvement with the Grade I-listed Bexhill Pavilion in Sussex began in 1991, yet the greater part of the project to restore and regenerate this iconic 1930s monument – designed by Erich Mendelsohn and Serge Chermayeff and opened in 1936 – remains as yet unrealized. McAslan and colleagues have been loyal to the project – despite protracted planning and funding problems, which have delayed its projected completion until 2003 – because this is a building about which they feel deeply. Mendelsohn's expressive and romantic architecture strikes a chord with McAslan and has had a strong impact on the latter's own work. Equally significant has been the cordial working relationship established with local campaigners, the Local Authority and Mendelsohn's daughter, Esther. When McAslan was first commissioned, the Pavilion faced problems both of serious physical decay and of adaptation to changing ideas of entertainment and leisure. To secure the funds needed to repair and regenerate the building, its perceived role had to change, from that of a local amenity to a regional arts centre, attracting audiences from a wide stretch of the south coast and its hinterland. So, alongside the much-loved theatre, there is to be a new gallery, reflecting an ambitious new exhibitions programme. One of the basic problems is that the Pavilion is relatively small – it was part of a far larger scheme, abandoned after the Second World War. Public spaces have been colonized for offices and storage. Some extension of the building – proposed by Maxwell Fry over forty years ago – was judged vital. The chosen solution is to construct a separate wing to the north, linked to the Pavilion at basement level, congruent in style but not a pastiche of the 1930s. While this awaits funding, the reinstatement of interior finishes and furnishings has shown the potential for recreating the dynamic ethos of a building which, over sixty years since its opening, still feels dangerously radical for the English seaside.

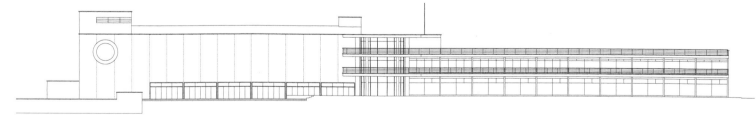

South elevation

Restored south staircase and terrace

[Overleaf] Terrace

Pendant light over the restored south staircase

Arts and Restoration

The Roundhouse   Like the De La Warr Pavilion, The Roundhouse is
virtually one of a kind, a rare survivor of early railway architecture with
an inspirational, if eccentric, history of use as gin warehouse, theatre,
rock venue and location for installation art. (Built in 1847 as an engine
shed, the building became redundant after only twenty years.) For several decades, The Roundhouse was in limbo, with no certain future, as
ownership has passed from one body to another and a succession of
proposed uses proved unviable. One proposal was to house the RIBA's
Drawings Collection there, but this would have filled much of the
interior with new floors. The advent of philanthropist Torquil Norman
appears to have broken the spell. Norman's dream of converting the
building for use as a young people's arts centre won Lottery backing
and is to become reality in 2001. The essence of the scheme is that the
great internal space of The Roundhouse will remain intact, with later
untidy additions that compromise the internal volume removed and the
historic structure faithfully repaired. It will provide a spectacular venue
for theatre, music and dance. Subsidiary spaces will be provided at
undercroft level, while the necessary services and access elements are
provided in addition to the original structure, clearly delineated 'ser-
vant' spaces in the Kahnian tradition. There will also be a sweeping
glazed dining extension and expressed glazed staircase tower signalling
the entrance on Chalk Farm itself. No attempt is made, however, to
ornament or conceal the dignity of the great brick drum. As at Bexhill,
the transformation of this historic survivor meant extended negotiation, with agencies such as English Heritage, on balancing literal
preservation against the vital necessity of new use. McAslan's proposed
additions are unaffectedly in the spirit of The Roundhouse itself – there
is no need for affected 'sensitivity' in the presence of an industrial
structure such as this. Inside, lighting, heating and other services will
not be glossed over. This is a tough building, which demands – and gets
– respect.

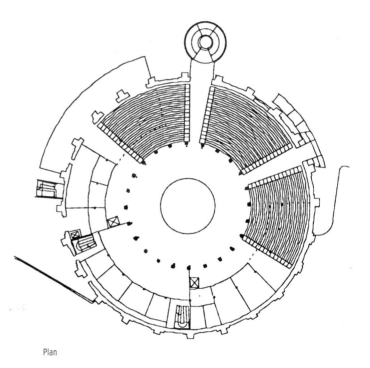

Plan

Existing space

Study model of the main performance space

[Clockwise, from top left] Creative centre in undercroft, main performance space, gallery and roof model

Arts and Restoration

78 Derngate Like Mendelsohn, Charles Rennie Mackintosh is an inspirational figure for McAslan. Despite its tiny scale, the adaptation (begun in 1915) of an existing Victorian terraced house in Northampton for the engineer W J Bassett-Lowke was the most significant project of his 'London years', boldly geometric in design and anticipating Modernism some decades hence. Bassett-Lowke was later the client for Peter Behrens's 'New Ways', sometimes claimed as the first truly modern house in Britain. At Derngate, Mackintosh worked within the framework of an existing domestic structure. The most striking external expression of his involvement is seen in the austere rear elevation, visible only from the garden and perhaps influenced by the work of Adolf Loos. The project is to provide a museum and education facility centred within the adjacent number 82 Derngate (a listed Regency structure) with number 80 carved out to provide a circulatory hub linking all three properties. The key intervention involves the demolition of a later extension to number 82 and its replacement by a lightweight and transparent entrance enclosure that itself relates to a vaulted workshop building set in a relandscaped garden. Here there is no attempt at sub-Mackintosh detailing, but rather a bold new approach that respects history without attempting to replicate it.

Garden elevation and terrace with Mrs Bassett-Lowke, 1919

Study model of the pavilion, terraced garden and workshop at 82 Derngate, with 78 Derngate on far left

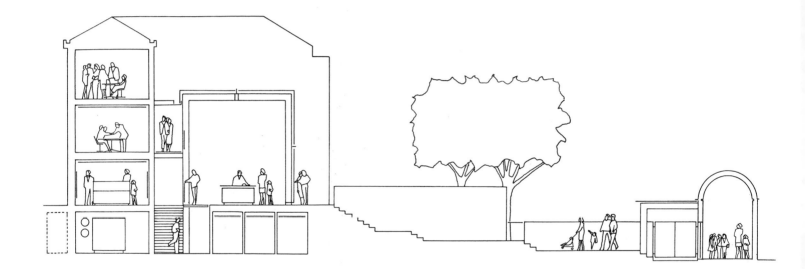

Cross section through 82 Derngate, showing pavilion, terraced garden and workshop

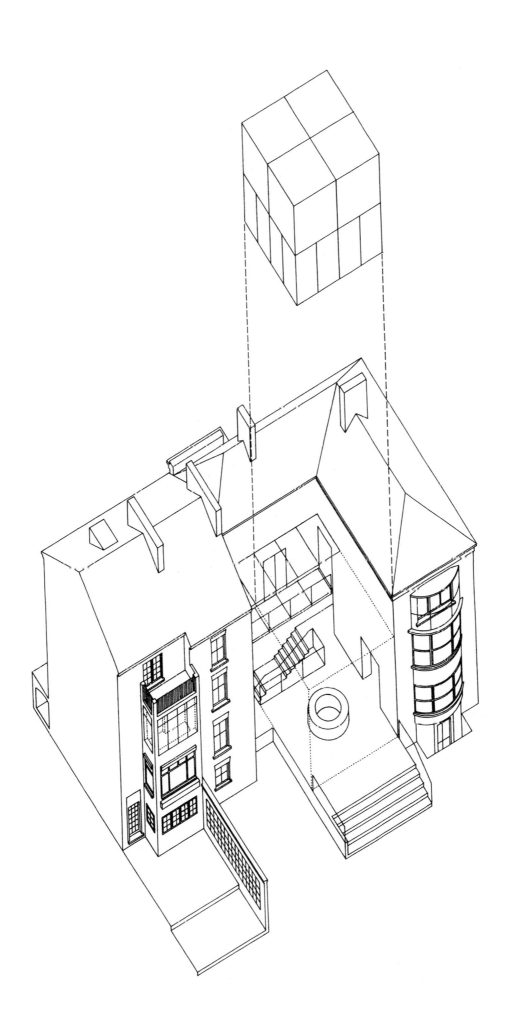

Exploded axonometric of the proposals and pavilion

Royal Society of Arts   McAslan is accustomed to working with classic modern buildings, but the RSA is a venerable institution, founded in 1754 to encourage 'arts, manufacture and commerce'. In 1774 it moved into purpose-built premises designed by Robert and James Adam as part of the Adelphi scheme. Its lecture theatre was subsequently decorated with heroic murals by James Barry. The RSA's premises (listed Grade I) have enormous charm, but by the 1990s they needed both a thorough overhaul and a strategy for future use. JMP's appointment in 1995 led to a masterplan for the whole complex, including comprehensive external repairs and adaptation of spaces. The remodelling of the lecture theatre (or Great Room) was a particularly sensitive aspect of the project. The space was technically re-equipped, the paintings conserved and cleaned and the seating replaced to a new formation. Central to the space's redesign was the introduction of a bold new glazed lantern, centrally positioned and justified as it replaced an original - long-lost - opening.

Great Room under construction

Remodelled Great Room

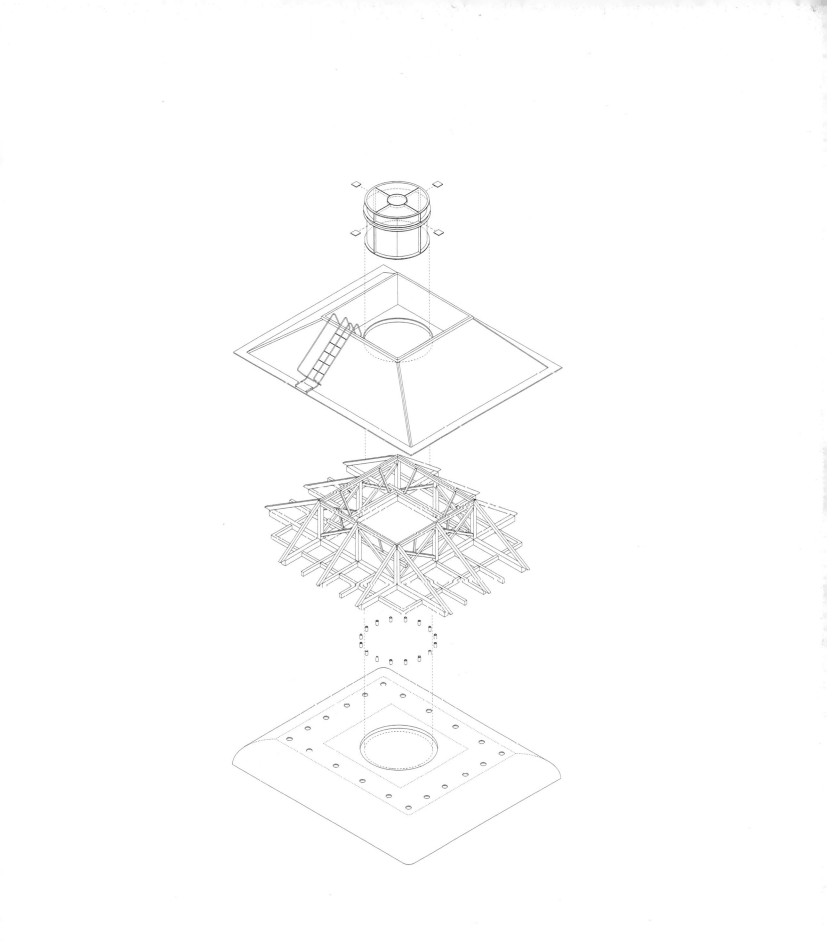

Remodelled Great Room through the new rooflight

Exploded axonometric of the rooflight and roof construction

Volubilis   Volubilis is a proverbial 'lost city in the sand'. Close to the city of Fez, it was a major centre of population and commerce under the Roman Empire, but began to decline in the third century AD. A severe earthquake sealed its fate: it was abandoned and not rediscovered until the nineteenth century. When McAslan visited Volubilis, reckoned the best Roman site in Morocco and one of the most significant anywhere, he was profoundly disappointed – there was no overall sense of history or place, despite the survival and excavation of striking remains (a triumphal arch, the columns of a temple and the mosaic floors of the villas of the leading citizen). The site was poorly shown – virtually unintelligible to non-specialists – and there were, local archeologists admitted, serious problems of care and conservation. Many choice items had been carted off to the archeological museum in Rabat, since there was nowhere secure on the site to show them. McAslan's project, developed in consultation with the Moroccan culture ministry, aims to present the site to visitors and to provide a strategy for protecting and repairing remains and a museum for artefacts excavated at Volubilis. The museum has Kahnian roots. The great vaulted halls evoke the monumental character of Roman architecture, but have views out to the site. There will be spaces for lectures and presentations and even for dramatized performances that bring the place to life. The cool restraint of the new building defers to the grandeur of the past, but is entirely modern in itself.

Volubilis, north-west quarter

Archeological museum proposed for the site

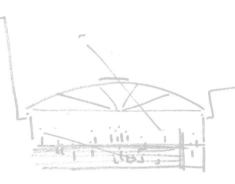

Peckham Square   Southwark is a borough in transition – from a neglected outlier of central London to a dynamic quarter, reinvigorated by the Jubilee Line extension and the Bankside Tate. The Local Authority seeks regeneration for the whole borough, of which Peckham is one of the poorest and more remote areas. The public square that formed the subject of JMP's 1993 commission is intended to build on the existing life of the High Street, offering a location for a market and for performances and public events and forming a gateway to a regenerated area, which includes a new public library. Relatively modest in cost, the single-span, forty-metre covered square makes a considerable impact on its mundane surroundings, and incorporates works of public art appropriate to the setting and a light sculpture by Ron Haselden, which is barometrically controlled to record weather patterns. In its unassuming fashion, this project demonstrates what the practice could make of more prominent locations, such as the South Bank (for which it submitted an undervalued competition entry in 1994).

Study model

The great gateway canopy

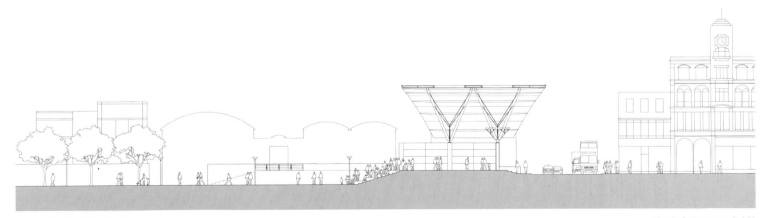

Cross section through Peckham Square

[Overleaf] The square at night

Ticket-hall roof being lowered into plan

Redhill station   This suburban station is a flawed gem. On the one hand, it offers a hint of the way in which a new architecture of transport could alleviate the general meanness of the public domain in Britain. Yet the scheme was only a partial rebuild of an inadequate old station and poor maintenance since its completion in 1990 has dimmed its brilliance. There are two main elements to the project, the ticket hall at street level and the platform-level waiting room with a retained linking stair between them. The architects undoubtedly had in mind the achievement of Charles Holden on the London Underground in the 1930s, but there is also a clear reference to the work of Mendelsohn. One is essentially practical, the other more poetic and expressive: architecture should be both. There could be no fundamental rearrangement of the station, just interventions into what existed. The waiting room is extremely lightweight, almost too delicate for the hard wear it receives. The ticket-hall block is more solid and monumental, a deliberate landmark for the town – the gateway to London, almost temple-like in effect. But the heavy Victorian platform canopies remain – and the train service is worse than ever.

Precedent: Southgate station in the 1930s by Charles Holden

Ticket hall detail

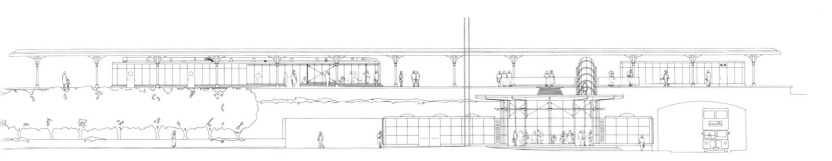

Ticket hall, platform staircase and platform pavilions beyond

Ticket hall interior

Platform building interior

Hounslow East station   The reconstruction of the undistinguished and inadequate station at Hounslow East, on the Piccadilly Line to Heathrow, is part of the continuing renewal process of the Underground system – which includes the new Jubilee Line extension, for which Troughton McAslan designed two stations. The brief for this new station was unremarkable in itself (it included ticket hall/concourse, staff accommodation and retailing). The expression of these functions has been given interest by being organized under a triple-vaulted structure that is Kahnian in inspiration. (A similar theme under-lay the practice's unbuilt, 1993 scheme for a London Transport training centre at Acton.) This rational model gives order to the diverse elements in the brief and provides a tough framework for intensive use in an unspectacular and scruffy urban setting.

Detail of elevation

Study model of vaults and linking sections

Study models

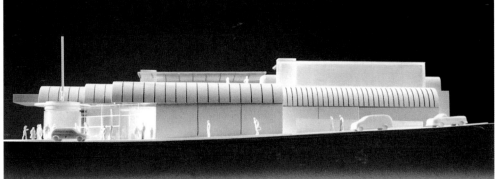

King's Cross station

King's Cross is the gateway to the north (and to McAslan's native Scotland). The station, designed by Lewis Cubitt and opened in 1852, is a magnificently straightforward expression of the 'functional tradition' of nineteenth-century architecture, a bold contrast to the elaboration of the adjacent St Pancras. The original diagram was extremely direct, with twin sheds for arrivals and departures and passengers accommodated in blocks along each flank, leaving the great arched front uncompromised. The rearrangement of operations this century led to the construction of a poor-quality structure in front of the main façade – replaced by an even worse design in the 1970s. The modern concourse is mean and overcrowded, while other spaces in the station stand empty or underused. Railtrack commissioned McAslan in 1997 to prepare a masterplan for development, in which improvements to passenger facilities would be partly funded by intensified commercial activity. Proposals for a Channel Tunnel terminal at St Pancras, plus the growing pressure on the Underground interchange, make an integrated approach vital – local bus services also have to be accommodated. The form of the proposed replacement for the 1970s southern extension remains undecided – 'a light and volumetric' design is envisaged. The abandoned flanks of the station will be revitalized, representing a return to the original plan's configurations. This scheme promises to be an exemplary combination of new build, intervention and repair in a historic setting.

The masterplan proposes the removal and replacement of the existing unsightly 1970s extension

Model of station extension proposal

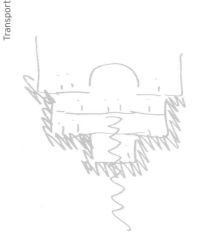

Ticket hall, with Oxford Street beyond

CrossRail, Dean Street station   The CrossRail project, as yet to be begun, is a vital part of London's public-transport strategy, involving massive engineering and construction works within the established context of central London. At Dean Street, the practice faced the issue of building within a Conservation Area in the dense grid of Soho. The new station had to have a convincing urban presence, while the development of the site above the concourse was part of the overall funding package. Daylighting the public areas of the station was a requirement of the brief. The design crafts a dramatic, vaulted, daylit concourse with expressed and stepped retail and office buildings above, adding delight, daring and some glamour to this drab section of Oxford Street.

Oxford Street over-site building and station entrance

Residential

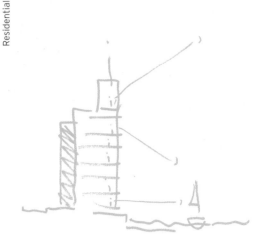

Princes Tower   McAslan's 1990 flats on the Thames at Rotherhithe reflect the antipathy of many young and innovative architects to the excesses of 1980s Postmodernism. Pseudo-vernacular styles dominated the active residential development scene in London Docklands at that period. In turning instead to Modern movement sources, McAslan invited trouble from the Docklands planners, who initially wanted something more 'in keeping'. McAslan stood firm and support from the Royal Fine Art Commission and other bodies allowed him eventually to win through without any compromise to the designs, which dated originally from 1986. There is an obvious hint of Mendelsohn in the scheme and the clean, white lines of the block evoke the heroic days of early Modernism. A decade on, the block still stands out on the riverside scene as a romantic gesture, homage to the past, but avoiding obvious pastiche.

[Above and right] Rotherhithe Street elevations

[Overleaf] River view

Original building in early use

Isokon Flats   The Isokon Flats in Lawn Road, Hampstead, now listed Grade I, were designed by Wells Coates in 1934. The building was the first block of Modern movement flats in Britain, developed by Jack Prichard for a discriminating and affluent clientele, which included, at various times, Walter Gropius, Marcel Breuer and Agatha Christie. The popular chef Philip Harben ran the Isobar, a restaurant providing meals for the residents. The apartments were essentially pieds-à-terre, reflecting the belief in a mobile, modern lifestyle. Even today, the block has a potent presence among conventional Victorian villas. It is a clear period icon, one of the most important Modern movement monuments in Britain. Yet it has degenerated in Local Authority ownership, both physically and socially, and consequently a decision has been made to put the entire block on the market. JMP worked for Camden Council on a masterplan for restoration – which was only partially realized. However, vital external repairs were completed and a start made on refurbishing some of the apartments, which are ideal for mobile, affluent Londoners of the twenty-first century. McAslan's commitment to the building has provided the basis for a full restoration that is now under way.

Renovated apartment interiors

Il Molino   Many architects (and their loved ones) gravitate to Italy and acquire holiday homes there, often in the favoured region of Tuscany. John McAslan chose not a conventional farmhouse but a disused mill in a valley close to the city of San Gimignano. Il Molino was intended not just as a holiday home but as a working studio. On several occasions, the entire practice has assembled there, spilling out into tents in the garden on hot summer nights. The aesthetic of the conversion respects the original fabric, and historic features, including the housing for the mill wheel, are conscientiously preserved. The key intervention was to form the great vaulted hall out of the existing structure, a move that McAslan credits to Jamie Troughton, who (with local architect Michael Goodall) oversaw the project's execution. New interventions and furnishings are of a restrained, contemporary variety, clearly expressed within the shell of the remodelled structure.

Garden view

Dining room and kitchen beyond

Main hall

Garden view from the main hall

The master bedroom overlooking the garden

Appendix The complete project list that follows describes and illustrates all of the practice's commissions since 1984.

It is organized in usage categories of operational/commercial projects, educational, arts and conservation, transport and residential projects.

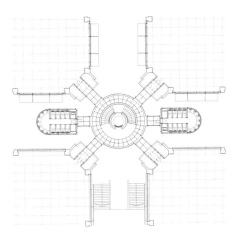

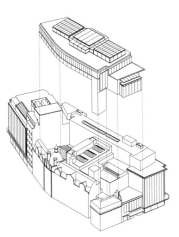

Yapi Kredi Bank operations centre
Istanbul

A recently completed 45,000-square-metre environmentally sustainable and low-cost corporate centre, Yapi Kredi Bank in Turkey houses 1,800 staff and comprises ten linked courtyard buildings in a campus setting, some 50 kilometres south-east of Istanbul. Administrative, operational, training, conference and social accommodation is enclosed by a series of fabric-covered internal streets. John McAslan & Partners, working with Arup Istanbul as project leaders, was responsible for the development of the entire project, encompassing briefing, masterplanning, architecture, space planning and interiors. The design was inspired by both Yapi Kredi's company culture and the covered markets and courtyard forms of traditional Turkish Ottoman architecture. It particularly responds to the steeply sloping site, which varies by some 20 metres across the development. The project was opened by the President of Turkey in 1998.

Client Yapi Kredi Bank, Turkey
Team Architect: John McAslan & Partners (Hiro Aso, Nick Eldridge, Adrian Friend, Andrew Hapgood, Martin Harris, Kevin Lloyd, Jan Mackie, Catherine Martin, John McAslan, Aidan Potter, Judith Quartson, Piers Smerin, Jamie Troughton, Roger Wu), Multi-disciplinary Engineer: Ove Arup & Partners, Executive Architect: Metex, Landscape Designer: Peter Walker and Partners, General Contractor: Baytur.
Area 45,000 square metres
Value £20 million
Programme 1994-98

Max Mara headquarters
Reggio Emilia

The headquarters for Italy's leading fashion house was the winner of an international competition in 1996, and is due for completion in 2001. Located on a 30-hectare agricultural site south of Milan, the low-energy development is intended to relate to its historic landscape in a distinctive yet timeless way. The design consists of offices for each of Max Mara's five companies, as well as showrooms and a 15,000-square-metre distribution warehouse set in an ecological park. Each of the principal buildings uses a Modernist architectural vocabulary of concrete, steel, brick and glass.

Client Max Mara Fashion Group
Team Architect: John McAslan & Partners (Umberto Emoli, Andrew Hapgood, Martin Harris, Jean Paul Jaccaud, Martin Markcrow, John McAslan, Roger Wu), Multi-disciplinary Engineer: Intertecno SPA, Executive Architect: Arcdesign, Concept Engineer: Ove Arup & Partners, Landscape Designer: Peter Walker and Partners.
Area 42,000 square metres
Value £35 million
Programme 1996-2001

Peter Jones store
Sloane Square, London

The phased refurbishment of the John Lewis Partnership's flagship department store, Peter Jones, represents the practice's most significant commercial project to date. World-renowned, the Sloane Square store is a distinctive landmark Grade II* Modernist 1936 building, which is to be sensitively altered to improve building services, operational facilities and upper-floor extensions without sacrificing its much-loved form.

Client John Lewis Partnership
Team Architect: John McAslan & Partners (Joanna Ako, José Aguilar-Garcia, Charlotte Anderson, Adam Brown, Umberto Emoli, Rui Grazina, Andrew Hapgood, Martin Harris, Martin Hopp, Scott Lawrie, Martin Markcrow, Ruth Miller, John McAslan, Ian McChesney, Grey McLean, Sarah Mitchell, Gemma Robinson, Gavin Smith, Murray Smith, Ryan von Rüben, Roger Wu), Structural Engineer: Hurst Pierce & Malcolm, MEP Engineer: Troup, Bywaters & Anders, Planning Consultant: Savills, Quantity Surveyor: Davis Langdon & Everest, Construction Manager: Bovis.
Area 30,000 square metres
Value £70 million
Programme 1997-2003

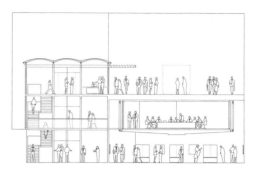

Yapi Kredi Bank headquarters
Istanbul

This landmark facility, which integrates such technological innovations as high-performance façades and energy-saving devices, incorporates a luxuriantly planted atrium garden and reflective courtyard pool. The building accommodates 7,500 square metres of trading floors, general offices and executive banking functions above ground level and car parking, servicing and secure areas underground, with a cultural facility on ground level. The scheme is due for completion early in the new century.

Client Yapi Kredi Bank, Turkey
Team Architect: John McAslan & Partners (Martin Harris, Martin Markcrow, John McAslan, Ian McChesney, Ian Troake, Roger Wu), Multi-disciplinary Engineer: Ove Arup & Partners, Landscape Designer: Edward Hutchison.
Area 15,000 square metres
Value £12 million
Programme 1996 onwards

Apple Computers headquarters
Stockley Park

The first major completed building by the practice was the two-phase Apple Computers headquarters and distribution facility at Stockley Park. Phase one of the scheme comprises 5,000 square metres of training, office and support accommodation on two storeys arranged around an atrium. Phase two consists of a linked three-storey mixed-use block of 6,000 square metres. The scheme was a finalist in both the 1991 Financial Times Architectural Award and the Civic Trust Award for Stockley Park in 1989.

Client Stockley Park Consortium and Apple Computers
Team Architect: Troughton McAslan (Martin Campbell, Jason Cornish, Bobby Desai, Nick Eldridge, Thomas Grotzeck, Joanna Green, Martin Harris, Jeremy King, Birgit Klauk, John McAslan, Nick Midgeley, Jonathan Parr, Stephen Pimbley, Aidan Potter, Judy Slater, Jamie Troughton, Mark Wilson), Project Manager: Bucknall Austin, Structural Engineer: Ove Arup & Partners, MEP Engineer: Mott Green & Wall, Quantity Surveyor: Davis Langdon & Everest, Construction Manager: Schal.
Area 11,000 square metres
Value £7.5 million
Programme 1989-91

Queen Victoria Street
London

Recently appointed by the Salvation Army, the practice is developing proposals for the design of a new office building. Since 1881 the site has been the headquarters of the charity; the current building dates from 1963. This valuable position is strategically located on the pedestrian route linking St Paul's Cathedral to the new Tate Bankside via a proposed Thames footbridge. The design exploits the historic location with a stepped form that responds to the local height limitations.

Client The Salvation Army
Team Architect: John McAslan & Partners (Martin Harris, Martin Hopp, Hannah Lawson, Martin Markcrow, John McAslan), Multi-disciplinary Engineer: Ove Arup & Partners, Quantity Surveyor: Davis Langdon & Everest, Development Consultant: Healey & Baker, Town Planning Consultant: Montagu Evans, Museum Design: Ralph Appelbaum Associates.
Area 18,000 square metres
Value £25 million
Programme 1998 onwards

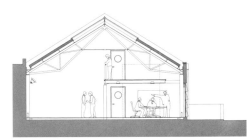

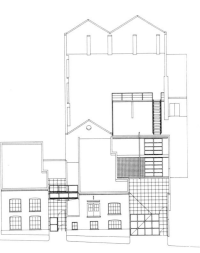

Thames & Hudson offices
London

The practice recently completed the remodelling of a 1930s warehouse building to provide
2,000 square metres of headquarters accommodation in London's West End for leading
publishers Thames & Hudson. In addition to
the refurbishment the practice looked at
space planning and furniture design for the
120-person facility. The project comprised a
rationalization of the building providing a new
multi-volume central atrium (incorporating
the company's 20,000-volume library), varied
office and studio accommodation, expressive
service cores, ducted air supply for the new
accommodation and the provision of power
for IT workstations.

Client Thames & Hudson
Team Architect: John McAslan & Partners
(Hiro Aso, Nick Eldridge, Martin Harris, John
McAslan, Ian McChesney), Structural
Engineer: F J Samuely & Partners, MEP
Engineer: Rybka Battle, Quantity Surveyor:
Boyden & Company, General Contractor:
Overbury.
Area 2,000 square metres
Value £1.6 million
Programme 1997–99

1-3 Colebrooke Place
London

A redundant, single-storey, steel-framed shed
was refurbished to provide studio accommodation. Colebrooke Place represents a fine
example of the practice's low-cost regenera-
tive work, which includes the insertion of a
delicately designed concrete-and-steel-
framed gallery.

Client Derwent Valley Holdings
Team Architect: Troughton McAslan (Martin
Harris, Kevin Lloyd, John McAslan, Jonathan
Parr, Jamie Troughton), Structural Engineer:
Jampel Davison & Bell, MEP Engineer: Ove
Arup & Partners, Quantity Surveyor:
Boyden & Company, General Contractor:
AJR Renovations.
Area 600 square metres
Value £400,000
Programme 1990

St Peter's Street
London

This award-winning and low-cost refurbishment of a Victorian industrial shed was
completed in two phases. Phase one provided studio accommodation on two levels
organized around a double-height entrance
area and extensively remodelled front
façade and interiors. The second phase
provided a glass-fronted, two-storey warehouse refurbishment with further studio
space, connected to the first phase by a
volumetric link.

Client Derwent Valley Holdings
Team Architect: Troughton McAslan (Martin
Harris, John McAslan, Malcolm McGregor,
Jamie Troughton), Structural Engineer:
Jampel Davison & Bell, Quantity Surveyor:
Boyden & Company, General Contractor:
William Green Builders.
Area 800 square metres
Value £300,000
Programme 1988-91

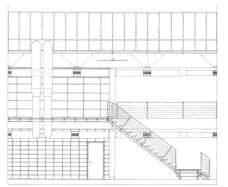

Rosebery Avenue and Hardwick Street
London

Nineteen ninety-two saw the completion of the practice's first major commercial development on an urban site. It involved the refurbishment of a 1920s industrial building on Hardwick Street and the provision of a new five-storey office on Rosebery Avenue, a total of 7,500 square metres of studio and office accommodation. The industrial-building remodelling created new vertical circulation and entrance cores with adjoining offices and studios. Part of the original structure was demolished to make way for the new landmark steel-and-glass building.

Client London Merchant Securities
Rosebery Avenue
Team Architect: Troughton McAslan (Bobby Desai, Madeleine Deschamps, Martin Harris, Christopher Mascall, John McAslan, Gary Mountford, Jonathan Parr, Stephen Pimbley, Aidan Potter, Piers Smerin, Jamie Troughton), Multi-disciplinary Engineer: Ove Arup & Partners, Quantity Surveyor: Walfords, General Contractor: Bovis elliott.
Hardwick Street
Team Architect: Troughton McAslan (members as above), Structural Engineer: Jampel Davison & Bell, MEP Engineer: J H Nicholson, Quantity Surveyor: Boyden & Company, General Contractor: John Nugent Construction.
Area 7,500 square metres
Value £5 million
Programme 1989–92

25 The North Colonnade
Canary Wharf, London

Troughton McAslan became the first British architectural firm to complete a major building at Canary Wharf. The sixteen-storey construction provides some 37,000 square metres of high-specification office accommodation. Built within a sixteen-month contract as part of the 500,000-square-metre first phase of the Canary Wharf Development, it is currently occupied by the Financial Services Authority.

Client Olympia and York, Canary Wharf
Team Architect: Troughton McAslan (Bob Atwal, Madeleine Deschamps, Olivia Fraser, Martin Harris, Birgit Klauk, Kevin Lloyd, Christopher Mascall, John McAslan, Jonathan Parr, Aidan Potter, Matthew Priestman, Murray Smith, Jamie Troughton), Structural Engineer: Ove Arup & Partners, MEP Engineer: Flack & Kurtz, Executive Architect: Adamson Associates, Construction Manager: Mowlem.
Area 37,000 square metres
Value £30 million
Programme 1990–92

Shepherd's Bush studios
London

Converting a three-storey, concrete-framed warehouse into a studio and office headquarters required major restructuring. A triple-height, top-lit central volume was created and all interior elements, including furniture and fittings, were designed by the practice.

Client Michael Peters Group
Team Architect: Troughton McAslan (Martin Campbell, John McAslan, Roger Meadows, Chris Perry, Jamie Troughton, Andrew Weston), Engineer: John Savage Associates, Quantity Surveyor: Boyden & Company, General Contractor: Wiltshier.
Area 3,000 square metres
Value £1.5 million
Programme 1985

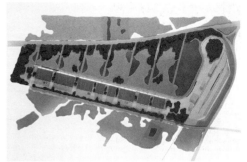

Design House
London
Commissioned in 1984 and the winner of a 1985 Office of the Year Award, Design House was the practice's first completed project. The 600-square-metre redundant car show-room was transformed into design studios organized on two levels and enclosed within a fully glazed façade.

Client Design House
Team Architect: Troughton McAslan (James Burrell, John McAslan, Jamie Shorten, Jamie Troughton), Multi-disciplinary Engineer: Ove Arup & Partners, Quantity Surveyor: Barrie Tankel Partnership, General Contractor. Roberts.
Area 600 square metres
Value £250,000
Programme 1984

Agora headquarters
Warsaw
The firm designed a competition entry for a leading multimedia group in Poland. The proposal suggests a campus plan of phased, low-energy buildings to accommodate the company's intended growth between 2001 and 2010.

Client Agora
Team Architect: John McAslan & Partners (Andrew Hapgood, Martin Harris, Martin Hopp, John McAslan, Pat West, Marek Wojciechowski), Multi-disciplinary Engineer: Ove Arup & Partners.
Area 35,000 square metres
Programme 1999

LIFE
London
Masterplanned by John McAslan & Partners, this vast scheme consists of 300,000 square metres of distribution facilities served by an innovatory rail-freight network. The site lies within an ecologically landscaped setting west of London and just south of the M4.

Client Argent
Team Architect: John McAslan & Partners (Andrew Hapgood, John McAslan), Multi-disciplinary Engineer: Battle McCarthy.
Area 300,000 square metres
Programme 1999 onwards

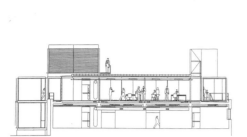

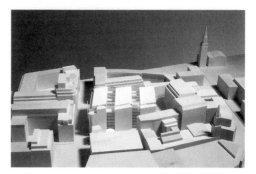

Soho Square
London

The project comprises the major redevelopment and extension of a building in Soho Square into offices. Retail accommodation will be situated on the ground floor and a dramatic atrium space is intended to mediate between the retail and office areas.

Client Derwent Valley Holdings
Team Architect: John McAslan & Partners (Hiro Aso, Martin Harris, John McAslan, Anna Wagner), Structural Engineer: Price & Myers, MEP Engineer: BDSP Partnership, Quantity Surveyor: Capita Beard Dove.
Area 8,000 square metres
Value £6 million
Programme 1998 onwards

Reed Personnel
London

Following a successful competition submission, the practice was commissioned to undertake a comprehensive refurbishment of an occupied Grade II-listed corner building on Baker Street in London's West End. The work involved the building's internal reorganization on all seven floors and an upgraded services installation to create environmentally responsive interiors with new finishes. Pre-existing spaces were fitted-out to incorporate customized, fully cable-managed offices. The basement accommodates an audio-visual presentation suite and the top floor a corporate apartment.

Client Reed Personnel Services
Team Architect: John McAslan & Partners (Hiro Aso, Martin Harris, Martin Hopp, John McAslan, Ian McChesney), Structural Engineer: Jampel Davison & Bell, M & E Engineer: Rybka Battle, Quantity Surveyor: Boyden & Company, General Contractor: Beck Interiors.
Area 1,000 square metres
Value £800,000
Programme 1997

2-12 Gresham Street
London

In 1996 John McAslan & Partners was invited to design a mid-rise, 25,000-square-metre office building for a financial institution north-east of St Paul's Cathedral and adjacent to the Grade I-listed Goldsmith's Hall. The proposal maximized the site's potential within the constraints of its historic context, providing flexible and efficient office and trading-floor space with cost-effective architecture. Gresham Street became a precedent for the practice's design for the Salvation Army on Queen Victoria Street in 1998.

Client Standard Life
Team Architect: John McAslan & Partners (Nick Eldridge, Martin Harris, Martin Markcrow, John McAslan), Structural Engineer: Waterman Partnership, MEP Engineer: J Roger Preston & Partners, Quantity Surveyor: Davis Langdon & Everest.
Area 25,000 square metres
Programme 1996

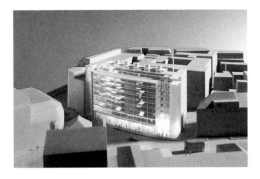

Premier House
London

Commissioned in 1996, a new and distinctive
150-bedroom hotel complex in Victoria
utilizes low-energy techniques and is
constructed in steel and glass. With its seven-
storey atrium plan, the building represents a
new generation of hotel design in London.

Client Derwent Valley Holdings
Team Architect: John McAslan & Partners
(Rui Grazina, Martin Harris, Martin Markcrow,
John McAslan, Raj Rooprai), Structural
Engineer: Price & Myers, MEP Engineer:
BDSP Partnership.
Area 10,000 square metres
Value £15 million
Programme 1996

Lange Voorhout
The Hague

The historic centre of The Hague was the
setting for a prestigious office refurbishment
project undertaken by John McAslan &
Partners in conjunction with Bos/Rosdoff, a
local practice. The completed scheme remodelled a listed seventeenth-century building,
incorporating new reception areas, common
facilities, circulation links, office accommodation and the design of a courtyard garden.

Client MAB
Team Architect: Fred Bos/Karl Rosdoff/
John McAslan & Partners (Adrian Friend,
Andrew Hapgood, Martin Harris, John
McAslan).
Programme 1994-96

West End Green
London

West End Green is a mid-rise, mixed-use
urban development of stepped building
forms centred around elevated courtyards
in the Paddington Green Conservation Area
of Westminster. Designed as a series of
interconnected buildings clad in a modular
treatment of terracotta bricks and
expressed concrete frames, the scheme
recently secured planning permission.

Client Waterfront Development
Team Architect: John McAslan
& Partners (Martin Markcrow, Catherine
Martin, John McAslan, Pedro Pereira, Jamie
Troughton) with Llewelyn Davies,
Structural Engineer: Buro Happold,
Quantity Surveyor: E C Harris.
Area 40,000 square metres
Programme 1995-97

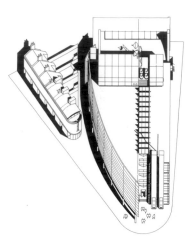

Middlesex House
London

A series of floor-by-floor adaptations around reconstructed cores constitutes the phased refurbishment of a five-storey 1930s building in central London.

Client Derwent Valley Holdings
Team Architect: Troughton McAslan (Bob Atwal, Hugh Broughton, Bobby Desai, John McAslan, Malcolm McGregor, Stephen Pimbley, Aidan Potter, Judy Slater, Paul Summerlin), Structural Engineer: Jampel Davison & Bell, MEP Engineer: PHD Associates, Quantity Surveyor: Boyden & Company, General Contractor: John Nugent Construction.
Area 4,000 square metres
Programme 1991–93

Bolsover Street
London

An extensive refurbishment of a Grade II-listed office headquarters in Westminster was completed by the practice in 1992. The project included the remodelling of the existing building fabric, the provision of a new circulation core and an office extension to the rear of the site, creating high-quality, fully serviced office accommodation.

Client Great Portland Estates
Team Architect: Troughton McAslan (Yasser el Gabry, John McAslan, Malcolm McGregor, Jamie Troughton, Mark Wilson), Multi-disciplinary Engineer: Pell Frischmann Group, Quantity Surveyor: Boyden & Company, General Contractor: Trollop and Colls.
Area 2,300 square metres
Value £2.5 million
Programme 1990–92

Lipstick Building
London

The competition-winning project for an office building resolved the complexities of designing a landmark building on a prominent corner site with an internal multivolume atrium and tapering 'flat-iron' form. The scheme remains unbuilt.

Client London Docklands Development Corporation
Team Architect: Troughton McAslan (Adam Brown, John McAslan, Aidan Potter).
Area 5,000 square metres
Programme 1991

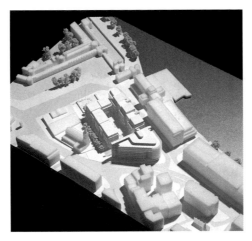

Princes Dock
Liverpool

The regeneration of Liverpool's historic Princes Dock (1820) formed the basis for the firm's masterplan. Focused on the redevelopment of commercial and retail space, the plan incorporates a rigorous arrangement of linked and independent pavilions.

Client Liverpool Development Corporation
Team Architect: Troughton McAslan (Hugh Broughton, Nick Eldridge, John McAslan).
Area 50,000 square metres
Programme 1991

Tower Place redevelopment
London

Troughton McAslan was shortlisted to design a major new office building on Tower Place, a site adjacent to the historic Tower of London. C T Bowring's 1960s buildings were redeveloped to achieve a total of 40,000 square metres of offices in a series of linked structures. The practice designed a series of four- and five-storey buildings with eighteen-metre spans around an elevated landscaped courtyard, with views opened to the Tower of London. All Corporation of London UDP policies were considered, notably the protection of strategic views.

Client Bowring Group
Team Architect: Troughton McAslan (John McAslan),Multi-disciplinary Engineer: Ove Arup & Partners, Quantity Surveyor: Davis Langdon & Everest.
Area 40,000 square metres
Programme 1991

Huntsworth Mews
London

Situated within a narrow mews in central London, the three-storey, single-aspect office building exemplifies a rigorous Modernist design organized in a linear arrangement over three floors.

Client Barry Tankel Partnership
Team Architect: Troughton McAslan (Kevin Lloyd, John McAslan, Judy Slater, Paul Summerlin, Jamie Troughton, Mark Wilson), Structural Engineer: Jampel Davison & Bell, MEP Engineer: Ronald Hurst Associates, General Contractor: Princeton.
Area 500 square metres
Programme 1990

Alexander House
London

Consisting of a double-volume, steel-framed warehouse and distribution facility and a three-storey, polychromatic-brick office building, this major new-build commission occupies some 2,800 square metres. The office building, in particular, responds to the scale of its surroundings with a bold Modernist architectural treatment. Alexander House won a Civic Trust Award.

Client Shilton
Team Architect: Troughton McAslan (Bob Atwal, John McAslan, Stephen Pimbley, Aidan Potter), Structural Engineer: Jampel Davison & Bell, Quantity Surveyor: Boyden & Company, General Contractor: John Nugent Construction.
Area 2,800 square metres
Value £2 million
Programme 1988-89

Pond Place
London

Concrete-framed and polychromatic-brick-fronted, the three-storey studio is set in a conservation area in West London. Despite its modest size, it became a controversial scheme due to its Modernist design within a conservation area.

Client Local London Group
Team Architect: Troughton McAslan (John McAslan, Paul Summerlin, Jamie Troughton), Structural Engineer: Jampel Davison & Bell, Quantity Surveyor: Boyden & Company, General Contractor: Heath Construction.
Area 300 square metres
Value £250,000
Programme 1989

Capability Green
Luton

Set within a parkland, the practice designed a two-storey, low-energy office building in 1998. The unbuilt project consisted of varied office space and became a precedent for the practice's completed scheme for Apple Computers headquarters the following year.

Client Lyfgun Properties
Team Architect: Troughton McAslan (Jason Cornish, Madeleine Deschamps, John McAslan, Malcolm McGregor, Jonathan Parr, Stephen Pimbley, Jamie Troughton, Mark Wilson), Structural Engineer: Alan Baxter Associates, MEP Engineer: William Sale Partnership, Quantity Surveyor: Howard Associates.
Area 3,000 square metres
Programme 1988

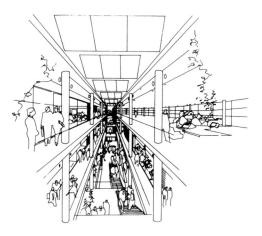

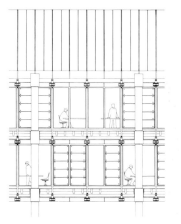

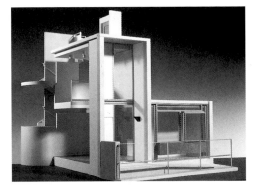

Petershill
London

On a site south of St Paul's Cathedral a six-storey, stone-and-glass office building with expressed atrium was proposed. Particular emphasis was placed on generating a design appropriate in scale and massing to the setting.

Client MEPC
Team Architect: Troughton McAslan (Bob Atwal, Martin Campbell, John McAslan, Aidan Potter), Multi-disciplinary Engineer: Ove Arup & Partners, Quantity Surveyor: Davis Langdon & Everest.
Area 35,000 square metres
Programme 1988

Allied Breweries headquarters
Burton-on-Trent, England

A riverside location played host to this unbuilt scheme. The design for the atrium headquarters was the practice's first major new-building proposal.

Client Allied Breweries
Team Architect: Troughton McAslan (Colin Mackenzie, John McAslan, Jamie Troughton, Andrew Weston), Structural Engineer: F J Samuely & Partners, MEP Engineer: YRME, Landscape Designer: Landesign.
Area 4,000 square metres
Programme 1985

Christopher Place
London

Completed in 1996 in a narrow mews in Euston, the specialist teaching centre for hearing-impaired children was the first of its kind in the UK. The practice attempted to optimize architectural and functional opportunities within the restricted site. Internally, the centre comprises audiologically controlled assessment and teaching spaces, which provide therapy for up to sixty children. Christopher Place was awarded a RIBA Award for Architecture in 1996.

Client The Speech Language and Hearing Centre
Team Architect: John McAslan & Partners (Hiro Aso, Martin Harris, Kevin Lloyd, John McAslan, Piers Smerin, Murray Smith), Multi-disciplinary Engineer: Ove Arup & Partners, Quantity Surveyor: Boyden & Company, General Contractor: Overbury.
Area 400 square metres
Value £640,000
Programme 1992-96

Educational

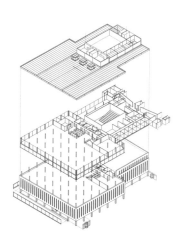

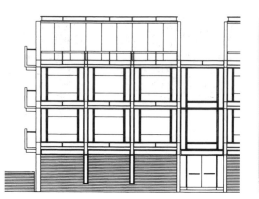

Imperial College Library
London

In April 1995 the practice was commissioned to design two independent low-energy projects: a 4,000-square-metre extension of the Libraries Building (including a music facility) and a 12,000-square-metre refurbishment of the Sherfield Building, both at the heart of Imperial College's campus in South Kensington. The Library involved extensive alterations and additions to the 1960s building, while maintaining the existing library's operational continuity. Completed in just twelve months, the project's objective was to improve services and provide upgraded and environmentally responsive interiors.

Client Imperial College of Science, Technology and Medicine
Team Architects: John McAslan & Partners (Hiro Aso, Nick Eldridge, Adrian Friend, Rui Grazina, Andrew Hapgood, Martin Harris, John McAslan, Karen Mitchell, Pedro Pereira, Nina Quesnel, Murray Smith, Roger Wu), Structural Engineer: Waterman Partnership, MEP Engineer: WSP, Acoustic Consultant: Sandy Brown Associates, Quantity Surveyor: Davis Langdon & Everest, Construction Manager: Schal.
Area 4,000 square metres (Library)
Value £6.5 million (Library)
Programme 1995-97

St Catherine's College Institute
Kobe, Japan

A new residential institute in Japan was the firm's first completed project abroad. The scheme comprises teaching, lecture, administrative and residential buildings in new and refurbished accommodation centred around a landscaped courtyard. The architectural treatment, based on a contemporary vocabulary, was inspired by the college's dramatic mountain setting overlooking Osaka Bay. The design was awarded the Anthology Prize by the Architectural Institute of Japan in 1992.

Client Kobe Steel/St Catherine's College
Team Architect: Troughton McAslan (Colin Glover, Martin Harris, Kevin Lloyd, John McAslan, Piers Smerin), Multi-disciplinary Engineer: Ove Arup & Partners, Construction Manager: Takenaka Corporation.
Area 4,000 square metres
Value £6 million
Programme 1990-91

Royal Academy of Music
London

Founded early in the nineteenth century, Britain's most established and celebrated music conservatoire is undergoing a remodelling programme by John McAslan & Partners. The scheme incorporates internal extensions into an adjoining 1820s Grade I-listed building on York Gate, designed by John Nash, which will become a museum, archive centre and practice and teaching facility. Within the courtyard, situated between the existing RAM and York Gate buildings and connected to both, a new barrel-vaulted rehearsal hall is proposed. This privately funded scheme is due for completion in 2001.

Client Royal Academy of Music
Team Architect: John McAslan & Partners (Umberto Emoli, Martin Harris, Jean-Paul Jaccaud, John McAslan, Ian McChesney, Magnus Strom, Anna Wagner, Matt Williams), Project Manager: Davis Langdon Management, Multi-disciplinary Engineer: Oscar Faber, Quantity Surveyor: Gardiner & Theobald, Acoustics Consultant: Sandy Brown Associates, Access Consultant: David Bonnett, General Contractor: Simons.
Area 3,000 square metres
Value £5 million
Programme 1997-2001

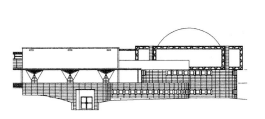

Florida Southern College
Lakeland, Florida, USA

A remodelling and new-build proposal for Frank Lloyd Wright's largest group of buildings, set in a citrus-grove landscape and built between 1938 and 1958. Work includes a masterplan for the 2,000-student campus, detailed analyses of and recommendations for the repair of key building elements and the development of a long-term preventive maintenance strategy in partnership with Ove Arup Research and Development in London and New York. Funding has been secured to undertake significant adaptive works and the first phase of refurbishment has commenced. It consists of the remodelling of the 6,000-square-metre Polk County Science Building, the last structure built by Wright on the campus. In addition, John McAslan & Partners was commissioned by the college to design a residential development for three hundred students, the first phase of which is now complete.

Client Florida Southern College
Team Architect: John McAslan & Partners (Adam Brown, Martin Harris, John McAslan, Matt Williams, Roger Wu), Multi-disciplinary Engineer: Ove Arup & Partners, Laboratory Planner: Earl Walls, Executive Architect: Lunz & Associates, General Contractor (Polk County Science Building): Kvaerner.
Area 6,000 square metres
(Polk County Science Building)
Value $8 million
(Polk County Science Building)
Programme 1993-2001

School of Oriental and African Studies
London

The University of London's rapidly expanding School of Oriental and African Studies (SOAS) in Bloomsbury commissioned the practice to develop a series of adaptations and extensions for the faculty. Stage one of the project (now complete) was a campus development plan that provided additional academic support and service space. Stage two, consisting of the design development of each of the projects, is under way. It is envisaged that Stage three, consisting of the implementation of the first of these projects, will begin during 2000, and that the entire project will be complete early in the new century.

Client SOAS
Team Architect: John McAslan & Partners (Hiro Aso, Andrew Hapgood, Martin Harris, Martin Hopp, Martin Markcrow, John McAslan, Ian Troake, Pat West), Structural Engineer: Whitby & Bird, MEP Engineer: EDA, Quantity Surveyor: Madlin & Madison.
Area 6,000 square metres
Value £10 million
Programme 1997 onwards

Imperial College boat club
London

Located on the Thames west of Putney existing boathouse, home to the club's Henley Regatta-winning team, is to be remodelled to provide boat storage, workshops, changing facilities, club room and student accommodation. A purpose-designed fitness-training centre will be based in a new adjacent building. Because of its sensitive site in a riverside conservation area the scheme has involved extensive consultations with the planning authority and local residents.

Client Imperial College of Science, Technology and Medicine
Team Architect: John McAslan & Partners (Hiro Aso, Martin Harris, John McAslan, Piers Smerin, Jamie Troughton), Planning Consultant: Montagu Evans, Multi-disciplinary Engineer: Battle McCarthy, Quantity Surveyor: Leslie Clark, General Contractor: Hunting Gate.
Area 1,300 square metres
Value £1.7 million
Programme 1996-99

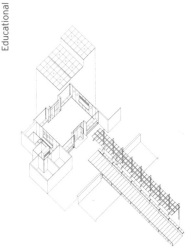

St Catherine's College housing
Oxford

The student-housing competition entry for the Grade I-listed Arne Jacobsen-designed college grouped 120 rooms and common facilities around a series of courtyards in a stepped arrangement of two-storey buildings. The practice had in the same year remodelled the porter's lodge for the college.

Client St Catherine's College, Oxford
Team Architect: Troughton McAslan (Adam Brown, John McAslan, Aidan Potter, Piers Smerin).
Area 3,000 square metres
Programme 1992

The London Institute
London

For the Borough of Southwark the practice developed proposals for a 2,000-student campus with 1,200 bed spaces and 10,000 square metres of teaching accommodation in Elephant and Castle. Consisting of a series of independent and linked buildings in a landscaped courtyard, the shortlisted competition design involved extensive consultations with the borough.

Client London Borough of Southwark
Team Architect: Troughton McAslan (John McAslan, Aidan Potter).
Area 18,000 square metres
Programme 1993

The Moat School
London

A project for the design of London's first secondary day school for dyslexic children and those with related learning difficulties was a competition winner in 1997. The scheme comprised the refurbishment and re-organization of a disused three-storey, L-shaped building in three phases, the first phase of which was completed in spring 1998. Within this phase the building was converted into a functional learning environment. A dramatic glazed link for public facilities will be installed in phase two, while the project's final phase will complete its varied teaching environment.

Client The Constable Educational Trust
Team Architect: John McAslan & Partners (Martin Harris, John McAslan, Matt Williams, Roger Wu), Structural Engineer: F J Samuely & Partners, MEP Engineer: J. Roger Preston & Partners, Quantity Surveyor: Gardiner & Theobald.
Value Phase one: £400,000
Programme 1997-98

De La Warr Pavilion
Bexhill-on-Sea, England

Appointed in 1991, the practice prepared a strategy for the long-term restoration, remodelling and redevelopment of the Erich Mendelsohn-designed, Grade I-listed building of 1935. The practice initially developed a strategic masterplan, resulting in the complete restoration of the building's external fabric. More recently a five-phased regeneration programme of the building's interiors has begun, the first phase of which has been completed and includes an art gallery, café and function room. Throughout the project, John McAslan & Partners has consulted with English Heritage, the Twentieth Century Society and the owner, Rother District Council, to achieve planning and listed-building consents. Substantial funding has been obtained from English Heritage, the European Commission Heritage Division and the Getty Grant Program. The practice has also been closely involved with the ongoing application to the Lottery to complete the remaining phases of the redevelopment programme that aims to turn the pavilion into a major arts centre early in the new century.

Client Rother District Council
Team Architect: John McAslan & Partners (Adam Brown, Martin Harris, Hugh Broughton, John McAslan, Ian McChesney, Anna Wagner, Matt Williams), Structural Engineer: F J Samuely & Partners, MEP Engineer: Rybka Battle, Quantity Surveyor: Davis Langdon & Everest and Maynard Mortimer & Gibbons.
Area 4,000 square metres
Value £10 million
Programme 1991 onwards

The Roundhouse
London

Selected after a competitive interview, John McAslan & Partners proposed the remodelling of The Roundhouse as a creative centre for young people and multi-use performance-art venue. The building, designed by George Stephenson and Robert Dockray in 1846, is regarded as an outstanding example of Victorian industrial architecture and is listed Grade II*. Originally constructed as an engine shed, it was converted to a liquor warehouse twenty years after its completion and was so-used for nearly a century until Arnold Wesker established The Roundhouse as a performance venue in 1964. Current proposals led by the Norman Trust focus on the adaptation of the building's undercroft into performance-related training spaces for music, TV, fashion and theatre. While the main volume will be remodelled as a flexible performance space for audiences of between 650 people seated and 2,200 standing. This includes the upgrade of acoustics, building services and performance-related technical equipment and the provision of much-needed ancillary accommodation.

Client Norman Trust
Team Architect: John McAslan & Partners (Adam Brown, Michael Durran, Martin Harris, John McAslan), Structural Engineer: Anthony Hunt Associates, MEP Engineer: Max Fordham & Partners, Quantity Surveyor: Gardiner & Theobald, Acoustic Consultant: Paul Gillieron, Theatre Designer: Scéno Plus.
Area 5,000 square metres
Value £11 million
Programme 1997-2001

78 Derngate
Northampton, England

The firm was appointed to develop a multi-dimensional arts facility in Northampton, the core of which will be a restored Charles Rennie Mackintosh house. Built for the toy-maker and arts patron W. J. Bassett Lowke in 1919, the tiny conversion of 78 Derngate completed Mackintosh's last commission. The project will also focus on the adaptation of the adjoining late nineteenth-century terrace properties (numbers 80 and 82 Derngate) into galleries, an education space, a café and support accommodation, with a linked connection to number 78. The existing properties have been purchased by Northampton Borough Council and the 78 Derngate Trust. The practice has applied for joint funding to the Heritage Lottery, to coincide with the submission for planning and listed-building consent. 78 Derngate is planned to open during the latter part of 2001, with its initial exhibition focusing on Mackintosh's link to Bassett Lowke, Northampton and Chelsea, where he spent his final years in England before settling in France.

Client 78 Derngate
Team Architect: John McAslan & Partners (Adam Brown, Martin Harris, John McAslan, Ryan von Rüben, Pat West), Structural Engineer: Jampel, Davison & Bell, MEP Engineer: Rybka Battle, Quantity Surveyor: Boyden & Company, Museum Design: Ralph Appelbaum Associates.
Area 750 square metres
Value £1.5 million
Programme 1998-2001

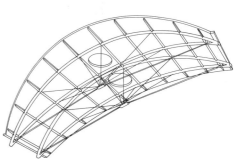

Royal Society of Arts
London

Early in 1995 John McAslan & Partners was appointed as architect to the Royal Society of Arts to remodel its five interlinked, Grade I-listed, Robert Adam-designed buildings in the heart of the City of Westminster. The development was carried out in phases over a two-year period while maintaining operational continuity. The first phase, the adaptation of the Tavern Room, was completed in 1995. Phase two was accomplished by the end of 1996 and involved the restoration of the building's external fabric and the extensive remodelling of the historic Great Room debating chamber designed by Adam in 1774.

Client Royal Society of Arts
Team Architect: John McAslan & Partners (Adam Brown, Martin Harris, John McAslan, Matt Williams), Structural Engineer: Alan Baxter Associates, MEP Engineer: Rybka Battle, Quantity Surveyor: Bristow Johnson, General Contractor: Costain.
Area 1,000 square metres
Value £2 million
Programme 1995-96

Volubilis
Morocco

The ruined city of Volubilis, founded in pre-Roman times and the ancient capital of the Roman province of Mauretania Tingitania, sits below the escarpment of Jbel Zerhoun in northern Morocco, near the holy town of Moulay Idriss, some 50 kilometres west of the imperial city of Fes. Excavations at Volubilis, which began in the late nineteenth century, continue today. It is the finest archeological site in Morocco and equal to any of the great ruined Roman cities that can be seen in Tunisia and Algeria. Its most distinctive feature is an astonishingly well-preserved basilica, although the complete triumphal arch, the columns of a Capitoline temple and a dazzling series of mosaic-floored villas are also memorable. As magnificent as Volubilis remains, the site would greatly benefit from further protection. The project investigates how this can be achieved through selective excavation, the partial restoration of a number of its architectural remains and the enhancement of the visitor experience with the design of an archeological museum displaying treasures recovered during the excavation.

Client Royaume du Maroc, Ministère des Affaires Culturelles
Team Architect: John McAslan & Partners (Martin Markcrow, John McAslan), Multi-disciplinary Engineer: Ove Arup & Partners.
Programme 1998 onwards

Peckham Square
London

During 1993 the firm was commissioned to design a new public square for the London Borough of Southwark. The square comprises three principal elements: a raised paved section adjacent to Peckham High Street providing a space for market-place activities and public events; a 35-metre-span, steel-and-timber canopy signalling the entrance to Burgess Park; and a smaller, paved area providing a quieter, less formal environment. The design was developed with two prominent artists, Alison Turnbull and Ron Haselden, who contributed to the surface treatment of the square and conceived a dramatic active-light sculpture that illuminates the canopy and square changing colour sequences that respond to barometric pressure.

Client London Borough of Southwark
Team Architect: Troughton McAslan (Hugh Broughton, Adrian Friend, Martin Harris, John McAslan, Aidan Potter), Multi-disciplinary Engineer: Ove Arup & Partners, Artists: Alison Turnbull, Ron Haselden, General Contractor: Costain.
Value £1 million
Programme 1993-94

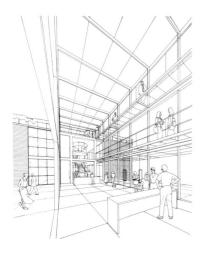

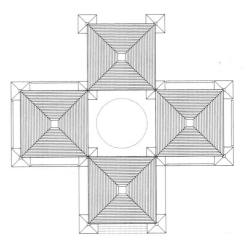

Ipswich Airport Terminal
Ipswich, England

The proposal consists of the adaptive conservation of the Grade II-listed, modular-steel-framed terminal building, designed by Henning and Chitty in 1938, while respecting the character of the original structure. The building will become a health centre incorporating crèche and nursery facilities.

Client Ipswich Borough Council/Bellway Homes
Team Architect: John McAslan & Partners (Adam Brown, Hans Grabowski, Martin Harris, John McAslan, Piers Smerin).
Area 2,000 square metres
Programme 1998 onwards

Hat Factory
Luckenwalde, Germany

With students from the Architectural Association in London, the practice developed adaptive re-use studies for Erich Mendelsohn's 1922 Hat Factory in Luckenwalde, some 50 kilometres south of Berlin. The building has been unoccupied for many years and has suffered extensive external modifications, which have dramatically altered its appearance. Working in collaboration with representatives from the town of Luckenwalde, the firm secured sufficient private funding to generate a strategic masterplan, which included the reinstatement of the building's external fabric and the analysis of potential development opportunities through the student programme.

Client Luckenwalde Town Council
Team Architect: The Architectural Association with John McAslan & Partners (Adam Brown, John McAslan), Multi-disciplinary Engineer: Ove Arup & Partners.
Area 11,000 square metres
Programme 1996

Trenton Bath House
New Jersey, USA

Louis Kahn designed this tiny work in 1954 and regarded it as his first significant project. Forty-two years later John McAslan & Partners proposed an extensive restoration programme. The Bath House consists of four interlinked pavilions constructed in concrete and blockwork with timber-and-steel-trussed slate-covered roofs.

Client Jewish Community Centre
Team Architect: John McAslan & Partners (Martin Harris, John McAslan, Raj Rooprai), Multi-disciplinary Engineer: Ove Arup & Partners.
Programme 1996 onwards

Commonwealth Institute
London

The company was commissioned to develop a strategic masterplan for the Grade II*-listed Commonwealth Institute adjacent to Kensington's Holland Park. The building and gardens, which were designed by Sirrat Johnson-Marshall and Sylvia Crowe, were completed in 1962 and formed the educational and administrative headquarters for the Commonwealth until 1995. In recent years, the building's role has become less significant as Commonwealth funding has been targeted overseas. Despite being one of the most significant public structures completed after the Second World War, the institute is in need of substantial remodelling and refurbishment. The masterplan focuses on improving the accessibility and legibility of the buildings, the animation of the gardens, and the prioritized repair and restoration of the building fabric.

Client Commonwealth Institute
Team Architect: John McAslan & Partners (Adam Brown, Michael Durran, John McAslan, Karen Mitchell, Piers Smerin, Matt Williams), Structural Engineer: Whitby & Bird, MEP Engineer: Battle McCarthy, Quantity Surveyor: Monro White Hilton, Landscape Designer: Edward Hutchison.
Value £7 million
Programme 1995 onwards

Hunslet Mills
Leeds, England

The Leeds Development Corporation and English Heritage asked the firm to prepare an adaptive re-use feasibility study for the pioneering Grade II*-listed flax-spinning Hunslet Mills. Designed by William Fairbairn on the banks of the River Aire in an industrial area and built in 1840, the mill is in a dilapidated condition. The study proposed a long-term regeneration programme, initially consisting of an arts-related lighting project, while providing low-cost, short-term, highly visible interventions to raise the profile of the derelict structure and to encourage the building's colonization. Three subsequent redevelopment phases were proposed, which would become financially viable once the commercial opportunities of the building were established.

Client Leeds Development Corporation/ English Heritage
Team Architect: Troughton McAslan (Adam Brown, John McAslan, Aidan Potter), Multi-disciplinary Engineer: Ove Arup & Partners, Landscape Designer: Landesign, Public Art Consultant: Public Art Development Trust.
Area 7,500 square metres
Programme 1995

Barbara Hepworth Museum
St Ives, England

The practice completed design studies for the remodelling of the Tate Gallery's Barbara Hepworth Museum in St Ives in 1994. Work included the provision of new entrances, improved ticketing and display facilities and accessibility alterations to the gardens and workshops to allow for increased numbers of visitors to the museum since the Tate St Ives opened in the early 1990s.

Client Tate Gallery
Team Architect: Troughton McAslan (Hugh Broughton, Martin Harris, John McAslan, Piers Smerin, Murray Smith), Multi-disciplinary Engineer: Ove Arup & Partners, Quantity Surveyor: Davis Langdon & Everest.
Value £150,000
Programme 1994

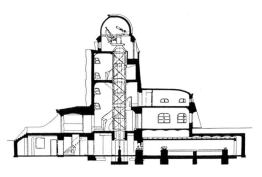

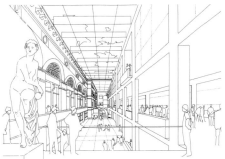

South Bank Centre
London

This project was a finalist in the competition for a scheme to enhance the environment of London's South Bank Centre. In the practice's outline, the existing unloved 1960s concrete elevated walkways were to be removed, a stepped landscaped park established facing the River Thames and a glazed winter garden introduced to link a number of its elements. The incorporation of significant transport connections was envisaged to ease pedestrian movement into and around the site.

Client South Bank Centre
Team Architect: John McAslan & Partners (Adam Brown, Martin Harris, John McAslan, Aidan Potter), Structural Engineer: Anthony Hunt Associates, MEP Engineer: Ove Arup & Partners, Landscape Designer: Peter Walker & Partners, Quantity Surveyor: Davis Langdon & Everest, Public Art: South London Gallery.
Value £46 million
Programme 1994

Einstein Tower
Potsdam, Germany

Working in association with the Astrological Institute of Potsdam, the firm completed a restoration programme for Erich Mendelsohn's celebrated tower design of 1924, dedicated to Albert Einstein. A detailed analysis and development of repair techniques for the decayed building's external fabric formed a major part of the project. It also incorporated phasing and building cost studies to achieve a fundable and operationally viable solution.

Client Astrological Institute of Potsdam
Team Architect: Troughton McAslan (Adam Brown, John McAslan), Multi-disciplinary Engineer: Ove Arup & Partners.
Programme 1994

Cincinnati Art Museum
Cincinnati, Ohio, USA

In 1993 the practice was the winner of a limited competition to masterplan new and improved facilities for this leading US arts centre. At the core of the project was a phased strategy to ensure operational continuity for the Museum, while integrating new and enhanced arts amenities.

Client Cincinnati Art Museum
Team Architect: Troughton McAslan (Adam Brown, Martin Harris, John McAslan, Aidan Potter), Multi-disciplinary Engineer: Ove Arup & Partners.
Programme 1993

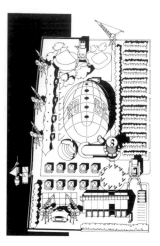

Legal Affairs and Judiciary Building
Victoria, Seychelles

A competition finalist, the design reinterpreted the local vernacular in a low-energy, Modernist vocabulary. The proposal was based around a series of linked two-storey buildings, which house the judiciary and legal affairs bureaus for the Republic of Seychelles.

Client Republic of Seychelles
Team Architect: Troughton McAslan (Adam Brown, Martin Harris, John McAslan, Aidan Potter, Murray Smith), Structural Engineer: Joe Pool Associates, Executive Architect: Tirant Associates.
Programme 1993

Monteriggioni
Tuscany, Italy

The creation of a small 'vest-pocket park' in the centre of the tiny, walled fortress town of Monteriggioni on a hill in Tuscany formed the basis of the company's design concept. The site is currently an underused public space just beyond the town's main square.

Client Commune di Monteriggioni
Team Architect: Troughton McAslan (John McAslan, Aidan Potter).
Programme 1993

Kobe Urban Resort Fair
Kobe, Japan

A 30-hectare masterplan established design principles for the Fair, organized as part of the Kobe Wakinohama Bay regeneration programme. The fair attracted some two million visitors during its six-month duration.

Client Kobe Steel
Team Architect: Troughton McAslan (John McAslan, Aidan Potter).
Programme 1992

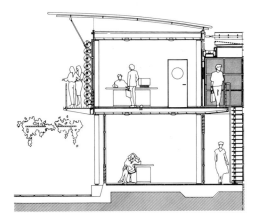

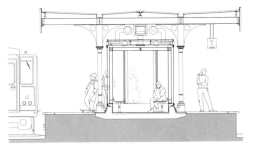

British High Commission
Nairobi, Kenya

Located on a hillside overlooking Nairobi, the new offices and varied accommodation for the British High Commission were designed as a series of discrete pavilions. The project represents the practice's first low-energy design and was influenced by a reinterpretation of Nairobi's late-nineteenth-century domestic and industrial colonial architecture.

Client British Foreign and Commonwealth Office
Team Architect: Troughton McAslan (Peter Beard, John McAslan, Aidan Potter, Jamie Troughton), Structural Engineer: Whitby & Bird, MEP Engineer: Max Fordham Associates, Quantity Surveyor: Davis Langdon & Everest.
Area 4,000 square metres
Programme 1989

Indira Gandhi National Centre for Arts
New Delhi, India

On the ceremonial Janpath route, the arts centre in New Delhi incorporates concert halls, theatres, galleries and research facilities. The scheme reinterprets traditional Indian elements in a contemporary architectural vocabulary. The shortlisted competition design was the firm's first major international competition success.

Client Government of India
Team Troughton McAslan (Joanna Green, John McAslan, Aidan Potter, Paul Summerlin).
Area 50,000 square metres
Programme 1986

Redhill station
Redhill, England

A new ticket hall and platform buildings for Network South East on the busy commuter line between London and Brighton was the first major transport scheme for the firm. The station comprises a circular ticket hall with adjacent retail facilities and glazed platform buildings, inserted below the existing Victorian platform canopy. In 1991 Redhill station was a prizewinner in the Structural Steel Awards, and the following year achieved the Brunel International Award for Station Architecture.

Client British Railways Board
Team Architect: Troughton McAslan (Kevin Lloyd, John McAslan, Stephen Pimbley, Jamie Troughton), Structural Engineer: Alan Baxter & Associates, Quantity Surveyor: Boyden & Company, General Contractor: Jarvis.
Area 1,000 square metres
Value £3 million
Programme 1989-90

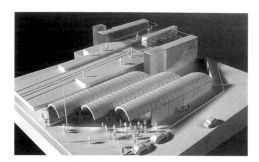

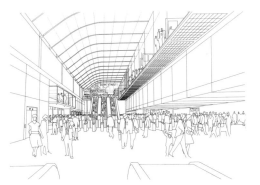

Hounslow East station
London

Serving high-level platforms above an embankment, the new station building on the Heathrow branch of the Piccadilly line is composed of a staff block, retail section and ticket-hall concourse, roofed by a dynamic triple-vault structure with a separate secondary support block. Two MIP lifts provide step-free access to and from the platforms. The existing structure is to be kept operational during the construction, ensuring the minimum disruption to services, with work due for completion early in the new century.

Client London Underground Limited
Team Architect: John McAslan & Partners (Hiro Aso, Martin Hopp, John McAslan, Magnus Strom, Pat West), Structural Engineer: Anthony Hunt Associates, Multi-disciplinary Engineer: LUL Internal Resources Team, Quantity Surveyor: Dearle & Henderson.
Area 640 square metres
Value £4 million
Programme 1998 onwards

King's Cross station
London

The initial masterplan for the redevelopment of King's Cross station focused on enhancing passenger amenities, rationalizing operational activities and optimizing commercial opportunities. Major remodelling of the Grade I-listed station will integrate better links with LUL, improve taxi and bus connections, provide a new concourse and incorporate substantial restoration and refurbishment within the existing trainshed. The project also aims to improve interchange facilities with St Pancras station, the proposed location for the Channel Tunnel Rail Link, and Thameslink services. The masterplan was finished in 1998, and the entire scheme is intended for completion by 2004.

Client Railtrack Property Projects
Team Architect: John McAslan & Partners (Hiro Aso, Adam Brown, Robin Cross, Hans Grabowski, Martin Harris, Martin Hopp, John McAslan), Multi-disciplinary Engineer: Ove Arup & Partners, Quantity Surveyor: Turner & Townsend, Retail Design Consultant: 20:20, Planning Consultant and Architectural Archeology: CgMS.
Value £50 million
Programme 1997 onwards

Dean Street station
London

The firm was commissioned to design a new ticket hall and oversite development for the CrossRail project, which remains unbuilt. The lower-ground, day-lit, volumetric ticket hall has its primary entrance on Oxford Street and is situated within the Soho Conservation Area. All operational facilities have been rationalized within service zones on either side of the ticket hall, allowing the 15-metre-high, vaulted passenger concourse to run the full length of the site, thus providing a clear and uncongested route between street and ticket barriers and escalator links with platforms below. The independently phased 8,000-square-metre landmark oversite programme above the station accommodates retail and office accommodation. The project has been developed in consultation with Westminster City Council, English Heritage and the Royal Fine Art Commission to make the best use of the site, while complying with statutory restrictions associated with its location.

Client London Underground Limited
Team Architect: Troughton McAslan (Michael Chadwick, Nick Eldridge, Adrian Friend, Martin Harris, Greg McLean, Murray Smith, Jamie Troughton), Multi-disciplinary Engineer: Ove Arup & Partners, Quantity Surveyor: Franklin & Andrews.
Area 15,000 square metres
Programme 1993-95

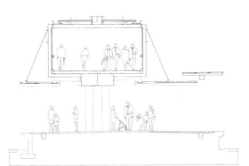

Canning Town station
London

Designed by Jamie Troughton, two new stations for the Jubilee line extension in London's East End provide passenger and operational facilities for Railtrack serving the North London line. The scheme comprises a six-platform interchange for London Underground, Railtrack and Docklands Light Railways, served from a three-level, reinforced-concrete viaduct structure with lightweight steel-and-glass enclosures for the Jubilee line and DLR ticketing. In addition there is an underground concourse that links the new London Transport bus station at ground level.

Client London Underground Limited
Team Architect: John McAslan & Partners (Christopher Egret, Nick Eldridge, Adrian Friend, Yasser el Gabry, Hans Grabowski, Martin Harris, Kevin Lloyd, Catherine Martin, John McAslan, Christopher Mascall, Greg McLean, Michael Pike, Raj Rooprai, Piers Smerin, Jamie Troughton, Roger Wu), Multi-disciplinary Engineer: WSP, Quantity Surveyor: E C Harris, Construction Manager: Mowlem.
Area 11,500 square metres
Value £30 million
Programme 1991-99

Stratford station
London

Troughton McAslan's second station on the Jubilee line extension is at Stratford. The new hundred-metre-long building for London Underground comprises operational, administrative and recreational facilities, together with three new canopied platforms. The new building and platforms are linked by a pedestrian bridge that forms a gateway to the new station.

Client London Underground Limited
Team Architect: John McAslan & Partners (Stephen Archer, Yasser el Gabry, Martin Harris, Ken Hutt, David Medas, John McAslan, Piers Smerin, Jamie Troughton, Roger Wu), Multi-disciplinary Engineer: WSP, Quantity Surveyor: E C Harris, Construction Manager: Mowlem.
Area 1,800 square metres
Value £7 million
Programme 1992-99

High Street Kensington station
London

The practice was commissioned to produce a feasibility study on the implementation of congestion-relief strategies within the existing station, while ensuring operational continuity was maintained throughout the period of construction. Short-, medium- and long-term strategies have been identified for creating a seamlessly progressive programme to tackle current and anticipated overcrowding problems and to enhance customer and staff environments, operational efficiency and historic architectural assets.

Client London Underground Limited
Team Architect: John McAslan & Partners (Hiro Aso, Martin Hopp, John McAslan, Pat West), Structural Engineer: Anthony Hunt Associates, Multi-disciplinary Engineer: LUL Internal Resources Team, Quantity Surveyor: Dearle & Henderson.
Programme 1998 onwards

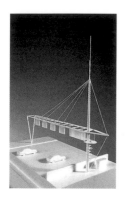

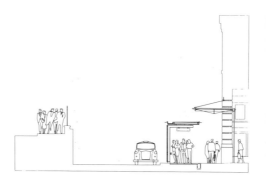

Motorway gantry system
England

The aim of the proposal was to replace existing unsightly gantry structures with new systems along a section of the M25 motorway, west of London.

Client Highways Agency
Team Architect: John McAslan & Partners (Nick Eldridge, Martin Harris, John McAslan), Structural and Systems Engineer: Anthony Hunt Associates.
Programme 1998

Access feasibility studies
London

In 1998 John McAslan & Partners prepared a feasibility study to assess the implementation of step-free and generally improved accessibility to six LUL stations, namely Pinner, Greenford, Hainault, Leytonstone, Newbury Park and Tower Hill. The study proposes options that meet the guidelines stipulated by statutory papers, in particular the Disability Discrimination Act of 1985, including new internal MIP lifts and pick-up and drop-off facilities externally. It is proposed to implement these measures by early in the new century.

Client London Underground Limited
Team Architect: John McAslan & Partners (Hiro Aso, Martin Hopp, John McAslan), Multi-disciplinary Engineer: LUL Internal Resources Team, Access Consultant: David Bonnett Architects.
Programme 1998 onwards

Heathrow Express Rail Link
Paddington station, London

Railtrack Major Projects and BAA commissioned the practice to develop the design of the facilities for the Heathrow Express service at Paddington station. The scheme focused on the design and implementation of various elements, ranging from the introduction of escalator links to London Underground to the construction of two new platforms with an on-platform baggage-handling facility allocated to the Heathrow Express trains. The work included close liaison with Westminster City Council, English Heritage, the Victorian Society and the Royal Fine Arts Commission, all bodies concerned with Brunel's Grade I-listed structure.

Client Railtrack Major Projects
Team Architect: John McAslan & Partners (Hiro Aso, Hans Grabowski, Martin Harris, John McAslan, Piers Smerin, Jamie Troughton), Multi-disciplinary Engineers: WSP, Construction Manager: Bovis.
Value £9 million
Programme 1994-97

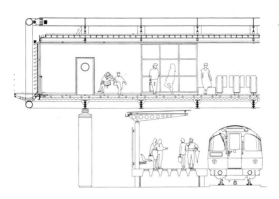

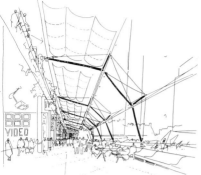

London Transport modular study

John McAslan & Partners was appointed by London Transport to undertake a station study in 1997. The practice investigated opportunities for modularization and standardization of components in the railway facilities.

Client London Transport and London Underground Limited
Team Architects: John McAslan & Partners (Hans Grabowski, John McAslan).
Programme 1997

New Cross Gate scheme
London

Bermondsey 'diveunder' for Railtrack's Thameslink 2000 project is a strategic infrastructure scheme designed to improve the opportunities for rail travel within London. By easing major constraints, the project makes possible rail journeys to a greater variety of destinations north and south of the capital. The structure at Bermondsey enables the two fast Thameslink lines, currently separated by the slow Network South East lines, to run side by side north of New Cross Gate, cross further lines from Kent and continue via London Bridge, Blackfriars station and Farringdon to St Pancras and north London.

Client Thameslink 2000
Team Architects: John McAslan & Partners (Hans Grabowski, John McAslan, Greg McLean), Engineers: Scott Wilson Mainline.
Programme 1996-97

Cardiff central station
Cardiff

The existing 1930s Grade II-listed ticket hall and Edwardian platforms were the subject of the practice's remodelling proposal. Of particular importance was the safe accommodation of large numbers of passengers who would use the railway station in the future. Cardiff's Millennium Station a short distance away, completed for the Rugby World Cup in 1999, will certainly add to the number of people using Cardiff central station.

Client Railtrack
Team Architect: John McAslan & Partners (John McAslan, Piers Smerin, Matt Williams), Multi-disciplinary Engineer: Ove Arup & Partners.
Value £3 million
Programme 1997

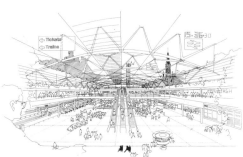  

**London Bridge station
London**

The introduction of the Thameslink 2000 project to the Grade II-listed London Bridge station formed the basis for a feasibility study undertaken by the practice. The proposal embraced the idea of two new platforms for the service, together with the necessary passenger links to platforms and the wider-scale replanning and remodelling of the station concourse. It has also high-lighted areas with potential for increased commercial activity within the station. Following this project, the practice was commissioned independently to design a series of bridge structures for Railtrack adjacent to London Bridge.

Client Railtrack Major Projects
Team Architect: Troughton McAslan (Hiro Aso, Adrian Friend, John McAslan, Piers Smerin, Jamie Troughton).
Programme 1995–96

**Elevated road and train system
Bangkok**

In association with Ove Arup & Partners the practice developed architectural proposals for thirty-two interchange stations in Bangkok, Thailand. Each station consists of a variety of ticketing, passenger, operational and circulation services within environmentally responsive building enclosures, ensuring that there was no need for artificial ventilation.

Client Hopewell Securities
Team Architect: Troughton McAslan (John McAslan, Piers Smerin, Jamie Troughton), Multi-disciplinary Engineer: Ove Arup & Partners.
Programme 1993–95

**Nescliffe footbridge
Shropshire, England**

Suspended above the A5 the steel-and-concrete footbridge was intended to highlight the significance of the link between adjacent villages.

Client Highways Agency
Team Architect: Troughton McAslan (Adam Brown, John McAslan, Jamie Troughton).
Programme 1993

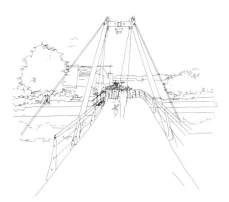

Acton Vocational Training Centre
London

An unbuilt campus incorporating workshops, classrooms, administration offices and a simulated working station for the training of London Underground staff, the project followed a two-stage design competition and featured a 200-metre-long, multivolume central atrium. The linear scheme was inspired by Scandinavian-designed, low-energy precedents, such as Arne Jacobsen's SAS Building in Stockholm.

Client London Underground Limited
Team Architect: Troughton McAslan (Peter Beard, Sharon Davis, Bobby Desai, Nick Eldridge, Yasser el Gabry, Colin Glover, John McAslan, Malcolm McGregor, Gary Mountford, Stephen Pimbley, Aidan Potter, Jamie Shorten, Zoka Skorup, Colin Smith, Jamie Troughton, Mark Wilson), MEP Engineer: Cundall, Johnston & Partners, Structural Engineer: F J Samuely & Partners, Quantity Surveyor: Nigel Rose & Partners.
Area 20,000 square metres
Programme 1992

Waterloo International Link
London

To accommodate increased passenger numbers generated by Waterloo International Terminal, the practice completed a 110-metre-long elevated pedestrian walkway for the Channel Tunnel Project, linking the International Terminal with Waterloo East station. Within the existing listed main station building, new escalator and canopy elements connect with an enclosed aluminium-clad, steel-framed walkway to Waterloo East station. During the construction process, operational continuity had to be maintained. One section of the structure was built in an elevated position and then lowered into place within a twenty-four-hour period over Christmas 1992.

Client British Railways Board
Team Architect: Troughton McAslan (Hugh Broughton, John McAslan, Jamie Troughton), Multi-disciplinary Engineer: WSP, Construction Manager: Bovis.
Value £2.5 million
Programme 1991-92

Leeds Corridors initiative
Leeds, England

A series of architectural, landscape, engineering and public-art interventions line the route of the proposal for the redevelopment of the motorway approaches into and through the city of Leeds.

Client Leeds City Council
Team Architect: Troughton McAslan (Aidan Potter, John McAslan), Multi-disciplinary Engineer: Ove Arup & Partners, Quantity Surveyor: Davis Langdon & Everest, Landscape Design: Landesign, Public Art Consultant: Art Development Trust.
Programme 1991

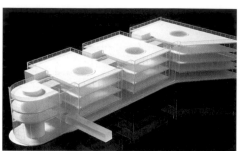

Park Royal interchange
London

Undertaken in conjunction with Ove Arup & Partners, the study established the feasibility of constructing an effective multi-modal interchange between London Underground's Piccadilly and Central Lines and London Buses at Park Royal in west London. The programme covered the
planning, architecture, engineering and cost implications for two schemes and has lead to the inclusion of the proposed interchange in the Local Authority's Unitary Development Plan. The potential for associated commercial development was also examined to allow a complete evaluation of the possible benefits of the scheme.

Client London Transport Planning
Team Architect: Troughton McAslan (Adam Brown, John McAslan, Piers Smerin, Jamie Troughton).
Value £15 million
Programme 1991

Waverley station redevelopment
Edinburgh

The revitalization of the station and its surroundings in the centre of Edinburgh focused on changes to the operational areas. The proposal also included the introduction of a major public space at street level and a significant retail and office structure, incorporated to fund the project and to provide much-needed commercial activity in the city-centre site.

Client ScotRail
Team Architect: Troughton McAslan (John McAslan, Aidan Potter, Jamie Troughton, Mark Wilson), Multi-disciplinary Engineer: Ove Arup & Partners, Quantity surveyor: Davis Langdon & Everest, Landscape Designer: Ian White Associates.
Programme 1990–95

Terminal 3 Heathrow
London

As part of Heathrow airport's development a new departures facility in the form of an extended wing was designed by the firm. An essential part of the unbuilt proposal was the integration of a significant retail component within the new facility.

Client BAA
Team Architect: Troughton McAslan (Adam Brown, Kevin Lloyd, John McAslan, Jamie Troughton).
Programme 1992

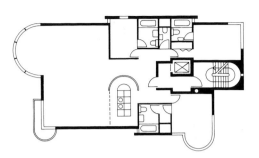

Princes Tower
London

Projecting over the south bank of the River Thames in the Rotherhithe Conservation Area, the eight-storey landmark apartment tower was completed in 1990. The award-winning design was inspired by Modernist architecture from the 1930s, notably the work of Erich Mendelsohn. The tower received major support from the Royal Fine Art Commission and Save Britain's Heritage, enabling it to obtain the necessary permissions for construction.

Client Private
Team Architect: Troughton McAslan (John McAslan, Aidan Potter, Jamie Troughton), Structural Engineer: Jampel Davison & Bell, Quantity Surveyor: E C Harris.
Area 1,100 square metres
Value £2 million
Programme 1986-90

Isokon Flats
London

Wells Coates designed the Grade II-listed Isokon Flats in Lawn Road, Camden, in 1934. In early 1995 John McAslan & Partners completed a four-phase masterplan based on the repair, restoration and remodelling of the Local Authority-owned housing block. The first phase of the work, completed in 1997, focused on reroofing, repairs to external elevations and balconies and the refurbishing of six unoccupied flats. The subsequent three phases will culminate in the building's complete restoration early in the new century.

Client London Borough of Camden
Team Architect: John McAslan & Partners (Adam Brown, Martin Markcrow, John McAslan, Karen Mitchell), Structural Engineer: Jampel Davison & Bell, MEP Engineer: Rybka Battle, Building Surveyor: Mellersch & Harding, Quantity Surveyor: Davis Langdon & Everest.
Area 1,500 square metres
Value £1 million
Programme 1995 onwards

Il Molino
San Gimignano, Italy

The Modernist-inspired conversion of an eighteenth-century mill is situated in a valley in central Tuscany and provides studio and living accommodation. The project, which included extensive landscaping, was the practice's first residential scheme abroad.

Client Private
Team Architect: Troughton McAslan (Adam Brown, John McAslan, Jamie Troughton).
Area 250 square metres
Value £200,000
Programme 1989-91

Publications

Practice profile
Financial Times ....28 Jul 1986
Blueprint ....Oct 1986
Architektura (Poland) ....Jun 1998
40 Under Forty (exhibition catalogue) 1988
Progressive Architecture (USA) ....Apr 1990
Blueprint ....Jun 1990
ICON Design+Architecture (Japan) ....Nov 1990
L'Architecture d'Aujourd'hui (France) ....Feb 1991
Country Life ....Feb 1991
FP Fusion Planning (Japan) ....Sep 1991
Baumeister (Germany) ....Mar 1992
Estates Gazette ....8 Aug 1992
Process Architecture (Japan, monograph) 1992
World Architecture ....Jul 1993
Building Design ....19 Nov 1993
The Sunday Times ....28 Nov 1993
Progressive Architecture (USA) ....Sep 1995
Tasarim (Turkey) No. 43 1995
Building ....6 Dec 1996
Building Design ....7 Feb 1997
Architects' Journal ....15 Jan 1998
Building ....16 Jan 1998
World Architecture ....Feb 1998
Architects' Journal ....10 Jun 1999

St Catherine's College Institute
Building Design ....8 Nov 1989
Building Design ....2 Nov 1990
Architects' Journal ....7 Nov 1990
The Sunday Times ....11 Nov 1990
The Sunday Times ....29 Sep 1991
Building Design ....8 Nov 1991
The Independent ....13 Nov 1991
The Times ....18 Nov 1991
Architectural Review ....Nov 1991
Blueprint ....Nov 1991
Kenchiku Bunka (Japan) ....Nov 1991
Nikkei Architecture (Japan) ....22 Jun 1992
L'Arca (Italy) ....Oct 1992
Okura Lantern (Japan) ....Dec 1992
Journal of Architecture (Japan) ....10 Mar 1993
Industrial Britain (British Embassy Tokyo) 1993
Best of British Architecture 1980-2000 1993
Building Design ....21 Jan 1994
Royal West of England, Academy ....Aug 1994
L'Industria Italiana del Ceminto (Italy) ....Oct 1994
Royal Academy of Arts 1994

Apple Computers headquarters
Architecture Intérieure Créée (France) ....Apr 1989
Blueprint ....Apr 1989
Techniques et Architecture (France) ....Apr 1989
Architectural Review ....May 1989
Building ....4 Aug 1989
L'Arca (Italy) ....Oct 1989
Progressive Architecture (USA) ....Dec 1989
Baumeister (Germany) ....May 1990
Immeubles de Bureaux (France) 1990
Ediciones Atrium SA (Spain) ....Oct 1991

Redhill station
L'Arca (Italy) ....Jan 1989
Building ....6 Oct 1989
Building Design ....10 Nov 1989
Architects' Journal ....13 Mar 1991
AJ Focus ....Apr 1991
Architects' Journal ....1 May 1991
Baumeister (Germany) ....Oct 1991
at (Spain) ....1 Nov 1991
Structural Steel Design Awards ....Nov 1991
Building Design ....25 Sep 1992
International Brunel Awards ....Nov 1992
Abitare (Italy) ....Dec 1992
International Iron & Steel Institute 1994
Tasarim (Turkey) No. 45 1995

Princes Tower
Architects' Journal ....16 Jul 1986
Architectural Record (USA) ....Feb 1987
L'Arca (Italy) ....Jul 1987
The Daily Telegraph ....23 Apr 1988
Country Life ....22 Feb 1990
BBC Design 1990 Catalogue 1990
The Evening Standard ....30 Aug 1991
aw architektur+wettbewerbe (Germany) ....Sep 1991

St Peter's Street
Building ....9 Sep 1988
Architects' Journal ....10 Oct 1988
Country Life ....6 Apr 1989
Abitare (Italy) ....Dec 1990

Shepherd's Bush Studios
Architectural Review ....Mar 1986
Architecture Intérieure Créée (France) ....Apr 1986
Interior Design ....Sep 1986

Alexander House
Architects' Journal ....5 Apr 1989

Pond Place
RIBA Journal ....Nov 1988

Il Molino
Country Life ....28 Jan 1993
Abitare (Italy) ....Nov 1993
Casa da Abitare (Italy) ....Aug 1996

Waverley station redevelopment
The Sunday Times ....12 Aug 1990
Architects' Journal ....29 Aug 1990
aw architecktur + wettbewerbe (Germany) ....Dec 1990
The Scotsman ....11 Nov 1991
The Scotsman ....14 Nov 1991
Sunday Mail (Scotland) ....10 May 1992
The Scotsman ....11 May 1992

25 The North Colonnade
Building ....21 Apr 1989
Blueprint ....May 1989
Fine Art Royal Commission ....Dec/Jan 1991
Building ....Oct 1991
The Times ....28 Jan 1992
The Independent ....1 Apr 1992
The Wharf ....19 Nov 1998

Uplighter
Interior Design ....Jan 1986
Architects' Journal ....25 Jun 1986
Progressive Architecture (USA) ....May 1987

Lipstick Competition
Architects' Journal ....1 Aug 1990

Acton VTC
FP Fusion Planning (Japan) ....Sep 1990

Capability Green
Building Design ....27 Oct 1989

Rosebery Avenue
Building Design ....2 Dec 1988
Estates Gazette ....8 Jan 1992
Building Design ....7 Feb 1992
Architecture Today ....May 1992
AJ Focus ....Oct 1993
AJ Focus ....Nov 1993

Indira Gandhi National Centre for Arts
Building Design ....13 Feb 1987

Design House
Architects' Journal ....25 Jan 1984
Interior Design ....Sep 1984

Baitlaws Conservatory
RIBA Journal ....Nov 1985
Creative Review ....Feb 1986

Colebrooke Place
Ediciones Atrium SA (Spain) ....Jul 1991

CrossRail, Dean Street station
Building Design ....22 Oct 1993

Florida Southern College
RIBA Journal ....Aug 1993
Sunday Telegraph ....27 Feb 1994
The Arup Journal ....Jan 1995
Building Renovation ....Winter 1995
Architects' Journal ....0 May 1997

Middlesex House
Architectural Review ....Nov 1993

Einstein Tower
Architects' Journal ....3 Nov 1993
Building Design ....5 Nov 1993
New Builder ....12 Nov 1993
BCB Journal ....Winter 1993/1994

Hat Factory
Architectural Association Monograph 1998

De La Warr Pavilion
The Guardian ....23 Nov 1991
The Independent ....11 Dec 1991
Building ....14 Feb 1992
Baumeister (Germany) ....May 1992
Country Life ....30 Jul 1992
New Builder ....6 Aug 1992
Building ....Dec 1992
The Sunday Times ....28 Nov 1993
Architects' Journal ....16 Feb 1994
Detail (Germany) ....Oct 1994
Baumeister (Germany) ....Feb 1995
Conservation Bulletin ....Nov 1995

Christopher Place
RIBA Journal ....May 1995
RIBA Journal ....Nov 1995
The Arup Journal ....Mar 1996
Architectural Record (USA) ....Nov 1996
British Construction Industry Awards 1996
Junior ....Mar/Apr 1998

Imperial College Libraries
RIBA Journal ....Feb 1997
Architects' Journal ....15 Jan 1998
AJ Focus ....Mar 1998
Abitare (Italy) ....Oct 1998

Peckham Square
RIBA Journal ....Dec 1994

Yapi Kredi Bank operations centre
Architects' Journal ....5 Dec 1996
Building Design ....7 Nov 1997
The Arup Journal ....Jan 1998
Architectural Review ....Mar 1998
YAPI (Turkey) ....May 1998
British Construction Industry Awards 1998
Architectural Record (USA) ....Mar 1999

South Bank Centre
Building Design ....15 Jul 1994
Building Design ....23 Sep 1994
Academy Editions 1994

London House
Building ....15 Nov 1985

Farm Place
RIBA Interiors ....Jul 1987

Manchester Olympic Tower
Blueprint ....Jul 1994

Regensburg, Germany
Architects' Journal ....10 Jun 1994

Nara Competition
Building Design ....7 Feb 1992

Hardwick Street
Architecture Today ....May 1992
AJ Focus ....Oct 1993
AJ Focus ....Nov 1993

Royal Society of Arts
RSA Journal ....Dec 1996
Architectural Review ....Feb 1997

School of Oriental and African Studies
Hiroba (Japan) ....Aug 1998

Isokon Flats
Interiors for Architects & Designers ....Winter 1997

Hounslow East station
Architects' Journal ....8 Oct 1998

The Roundhouse
Architects' Journal ....8 May 1997
Building Design ....5 Dec 1997
The Sunday Telegraph ....8 Feb 1998
The Times ....18 May 1998
The Independent ....25 Nov 1998
The Times ....25 Nov 1998
The Financial Times ....25 Nov 1998
Architects' Journal ....26 Nov 1998

Peter Jones store
Building Design ....5 Jun 1998

Queen Victoria Street
The Times ....7 Aug 1998

Canning Town station
Building Design ....23 Oct 1992
Building ....14 Feb 1997
Architectural Review ....May 1999

Photography Credits

Peter Cook 2, 19-25, 33, 44-45, 49-55, 57-59, 61-63, 65, 68-69, 71-75, 77, 79-81, 99 [top right], 102-03, 113-14, 119-21, 139-43
Alan Delaney 18, 76, 112
Andrew Putler/Richard Armiger/Network Modelbuilders 26-27, 37-39, 78, 82, 89-90, 94-95, 106-07, 109, 129
Acdesign 29-30
Michael Dyer & Associates/Richard Armiger/Network Modelbuilders 34
Alistair Hunter 46-47
Richard Bryant 66-67, 99 [bottom left], 100-01, 136-37
Hiroyuki Hirai 83, 85-87
Dan McCrie 117
Robin Barton 134-35
Andrew Putler/James Wink Modelbuilder 43
Andrew Putler/Martin Harris Modelbuilder 97, 118
Martin Charles 123-27
Andrew Putler/Martin Harris/Network Modelbuilders 131-33